Grandma's Wartime Baking Book

ALSO BY JOANNE LAMB HAYES

Grandma's Wartime Kitchen

(WITH LORI STEIN)
Recipes from America's Small Farms

(WITH BONNIE TANDY LEBLANG)
Grains
Beans
365 Great Cookies and Brownies
Rice
Country Entertaining
The Weekend Kitchen

Grandma's Wartime Baking Book

World War II
and the Way We Baked

Joanne Lamb Hayes

ST. MARTIN'S PRESS ✺ NEW YORK

Posters reproduced courtesy of Northwestern University Library
http://www.library.northwesu/govpub/collections/wwii-posters/index.html

www.stmartins.com

Book design and composition by Victoria Kuskowski

Library of Congress Cataloging-in-Publication Data

Hayes, Joanne Lamb.
  Grandma's wartime baking book: World War II and the way we baked / Joanne Lamb Hayes.
    p. cm.
  ISBN 0-312-30628-8
    1. Baking—History—20th century. 2. World War, 1939–1945—Food supply—United States. I. Title.

TX765.H385 2003
641.8'15'0973'09045—dc21   2003052603

First Edition: November 2003

10 9 8 7 6 5 4 3 2 1

In memory of

Hilda Lanhardt Hayes,

a wonderful friend who taught me

much about baking

★ ★ ★ ★ ★ ★

Contents

★ ★ ★ ★ ★ ★ ★ ★ ★ ★ ★ ★

Acknowledgments

My thanks to:

Dorothy Leese Lamb, my mother, for her continued support in all I do. The more I learn about the 1940s homemaker, the more I admire her stamina.

Heather and Jonathan Nanberg, and Claire and Tyson Lewis, my children, who never complained when all they could find at Mom's house for nearly a year was bread and dessert.

Angela Miller, my agent, for her enthusiasm for the project and for always being there when I had a question.

Marian Lizzi, my editor, and the staff at St. Martin's Press for wanting to know more about my favorite subject and for making the book the best it could be.

Beth Clausen and the staff at Northwestern University Library for their help with the wonderful World War II posters.

Introduction

Three years ago when I wrote *Grandma's Wartime Kitchen: World War II and the Way We Cooked*, I was especially fascinated by the creative ways wartime homemakers were able to provide baked treats for their families. My baking files bulged with wonderful things that there just wasn't room to include in that book, which focused on all the problems home cooks faced "for the duration." As I spoke to groups about the wartime kitchen, I found that many of the questions and fond reminiscences involved the baked goods that had been produced despite the shortages of pantry supplies and the rationing of sugar, butter, and canned goods. This book is a nostalgic look at those cakes, pies, cookies, breads, and baked desserts that raised spirits on the home front and the special treats that traveled thousands of miles in order to bring familiar flavors to Americans fighting the war abroad.

When Japan bombed Pearl Harbor on December 7, 1941, the aggressor and the location of the attack were a surprise to most Americans, but the fact that the country was going to war was not totally unexpected. World War II had officially started on September 1, 1939, when Germany invaded Poland; Britain and France declared war two days later, on September 3. Americans, still battered by the worst of financial times, fervently hoped that the country could stay neutral, but by early 1941 it was necessary to start humanitarian aid to Britain through the Lend-Lease Act. Soon German submarines interfered with shipping on the East Coast of the United States and the possibility of war threatened.

The twentieth century had already produced great changes in the lives of American women, but the next three and a half years were going to rewrite the rules more dramatically than anything they had seen yet. Until that time, working-class women had

Do with less— so they'll have enough!

RATIONING GIVES YOU YOUR FAIR SHARE

been employed mostly in factory or domestic jobs and middle-class women managed the home, usually with the help of at least one maid or cook. At the onset of the war, the government suddenly encouraged all women to think of their work as war work and to improve the nutritional status of their family and volunteer for Red Cross work, war bond drives, civil defense posts, and community activities. Soon the support of programs such as rationing and Victory Gardening became part of their responsibility as well. Working-class women who had previously held low-paying factory and domestic jobs could suddenly fill the positions in industry vacated by men entering the armed forces— and received a much improved salary. Middle-class women took over unaccustomed work in the home, as domestic help was no longer available, and soon took over office, factory, and farm work as well. Nearly half of all American women held a job at some point during the war. Whereas in peacetime employed women were mostly young and unmarried, during the war three-quarters of the increase in women's employment was made up of married women.

As women took on more responsibilities, government public relations campaigns and the media that they looked to for guidance offered no leeway in household standards. After a 10- to 12-hour defense plant shift, wartime homemakers were expected to put a nutritious meal on an impeccably linen-clad table, have the kitchen spotless in no time, tidy up the victory garden or can a few quarts of vegetables, and pack and refrigerate hearty lunches for the next day, all the while stylishly clothed in a dress and apron made over from last year's outfits. Home-front warriors tackled this challenge with stamina. When told they could do more, they did.

The inflation and food shortages of World War I were not forgotten in 1941. The American government tried to implement price controls before the country entered the war and were finally able to achieve it by October 1942. In the meantime, national surveys had shown that a majority of Americans preferred rationing to the chaos produced during the previous war and wanted to make sure that food would be available to everyone. In January of 1942, the Office of Price Administration named volunteer local boards to oversee the program. Eventually there were ten rationing programs. Food rationing began on May 5, 1942, with the 28-stamp "sugar book" and went on to include coffee, butter and other fats, canned and frozen goods, and red meat by February of 1943. Because of the different nature of the products rationed there were eventually four different ways of granting permission to buy—Certificate Rationing (for equipment and metal goods), Differential Coupon Rationing (for items such as gasoline and oil that some people needed more than others), Uniform Coupon Rationing (for commodities like sugar and coffee that did not vary greatly within the category), and Point Rationing (for items such as protein sources, fats and canned goods that did vary—e.g., more desirable cuts of meat "cost" more points). Constant media attention and the Home-Front Pledge that homemakers were encouraged to take reminded everyone that it was important to fight inflation and to avoid black-market goods.

Although a cup of rationed coffee would have been the perfect partner for most of the treats in this book, sugar and butter rationing had the greatest impact on baked goods.

The rationing and unpredictable availability of canned fruit and milk products made items such as Pineapple Upside-Down Cake and sweetened condensed milk frostings extra special when they were available. Most of the recipes in this book call for "vegetable shortening or butter (or a mixture)." When the government limited the amount of all animal fats on the home front because they were needed for the production of glycerin, they encouraged vegetable shortening producers to fill the home baker's need for fats with their products. Although butter was preferred, vegetable shortening was available and was widely used. Today, there is no shortage of butter and you can make the decision on the basis of personal preference or cost. In many of the recipes you wouldn't be able to tell the difference, but when making cakes and cookies you might want to think about the decision. I would suggest choosing butter for all cakes because it gives a noticeable buttery flavor (unless they contain molasses, which will hide the flavor) and produces a finer texture. Cookies made with butter will spread more and become crisper than cookies made with shortening, but they will be more fragile for shipping.

Except for special occasions, the home-front baker used a variety of substitutes for white granulated sugar. If the choice was brown sugar, the recipe could remain very similar to one that would have been made with granulated sugar. Brown sugar added moisture, a mellower color, and acid that was often counteracted by adding a little baking soda instead of all baking powder. When molasses, honey, maple syrup, or corn syrup were used, the liquid in the recipe had to be adjusted to take into consideration the liquid added by the sweetener. With the exception of the corn syrup, the product added its distinct flavor as well as sweetness. Light corn syrup added no flavor but was less sweet than the other options. In general, the use of substitutes for granulated sugar produced products that were denser and coarser in texture, and less sweet.

Throughout the book, you will find recipes that are labeled "Wartime Special." While these recipes may not be a first choice to bake today, they are all examples of creative solutions to the problems posed by rationing and scarcity, and of the willingness of the home-front baker to make use of whatever was on the grocer's shelf or her own cupboard to bring something interesting to her family's table.

It is surprising how similar the concerns expressed by today's family cooks (both men and women) are to the problems faced by the home-front food providers during World War II—finding quick and easy recipes that will provide the right nutrition to keep their families healthy. There weren't as many prepared foods and mixes available in the 1940s as there are now, and women had busy schedules then too—the quick tricks they discovered for preparing family-pleasing baked goods work just as well today as they did years ago. In addition, these tasty desserts have the advantages of being made mostly from simple, chemical-free ingredients and of being relatively low in fat and refined sugar.

Portion sizes were smaller in the 1940s than they are today. Pie plates and muffin tins were shallower, and a standard cupcake was about 1½ inches tall. The serving sizes given in this book reflect those standards, but that doesn't mean you can't cut breads, cakes, and pies into fewer pieces or bake muffins and cupcakes in 8 or 10 cups rather than 12.

As I began testing the recipes in this book, I remembered watching my mother or grandmother take a few minutes away from their wartime work to stir together some nutritious natural ingredients, pour the mixture into a well-used pan, and place it in the oven. Soon the delicious aroma filled the house and everyone knew that whether or not there was meat, butter, sugar, or coffee on the table, something wonderful was coming from the oven. It really hadn't taken much time and the reward was phenomenal. As everyone came home, tired from their extra responsibilities, they were welcomed by the promise of something good to look forward to—all was well within our four walls and perhaps soon with the world.

★ ★ ★ ★ ★ Victory Cakes ★ ★ ★ ★ ★

CELEBRATION LAYERS AND LOAVES

"Cocoanut" Cake	Raisin Fruitcake
Creole Layer Cake	Red Devil's Food Cake
Ginger-Raisin Cake	Service Cake
Harvest Cake	Sugarless Chocolate Cake
Hurry Scurry Cake	Sweet Potato Victory Cake
Jiffy Cake	Three-Way Cake
Lafayette Gingerbread	War Cake
Mincemeat Fruit Cake	Wedding Cake
Molasses Bread Crumb Cake	

WARTIME SPECIAL

Blueberry-Honey Cake

A HOMEMADE CAKE for dessert makes an occasion out of an ordinary meal. Through the busiest and the hardest of times, American bakers have always found a way to create these comforting sweets for families and friends. "War" cakes and "Victory" cakes were developed during World War I, and those recipes were still a part of the repertoire of most home bakers when it again became necessary to find recipes that limited the use of ingredients that were difficult to find as well as those that were rationed. The terms are applied to many recipes; the main criteria was that they substitute ingredients that are likely to be available for those that are scarce or rationed. They represent creativity derived from necessity, and sometimes the comforting flavors that result make the cake a permanent part of our national culinary heritage.

One of the biggest helps home bakers had in coping with the uneven availability of ingredients was the great variety of cake recipes that were developed to deal with different shortages. There were cakes that used corn syrup, honey, maple syrup, molasses, brown sugar, boiled raisins, the heavy syrup from canned foods, and other commercially sweetened products in place of sugar. While most cake recipes substituted vegetable shortening for butter, there were some cakes that called for vegetable oil, lard, or chicken fat. Because sugar and fat are the ingredients that make baked products tender, most recipes were only severely restricted in one or the other in the hopes that if the baker was low on sugar, there was a little extra shortening in the house that week and the recipe higher in fat could be used. Recipes using no eggs are likely to have been carried over from the First World War, when eggs were less available. During World War II, there was an adequate supply of eggs nationwide, but those recipes were still useful because local distribution was sometimes a problem. And, with gasoline rationed, it was impractical to drive around to find a grocer who had the item you were missing if you could do without it.

During the war it was especially important to have a cake for celebrations. Magazine articles on entertaining and food advertisements often showed servicemen and their dates around an attractively set table with only a cake in the center. If the occasion was a wedding, the Christmas holiday, or a long-awaited furlough, it was often celebrated with a special cake made to prewar standards, even if the whole family had to pool ration coupons to get the sugar and butter. On other holidays, a molasses-sweetened treat decorated for the day was the star. Pound cake was the one cake that seemed to disappear "for the duration," probably because it called for a pound of butter and a pound of sugar.

Most World War II cake bakers still remembered a time when cake baking was unpredictable because of the poorly formulated baking powders on the market. By the 1940s, baking powder was standardized and fairly reliable, making one-bowl and mixer cakes possible. Their success was a big help to busy homemakers. The cakes that follow are based on ones that appeared in pamphlets and periodicals of the period. Although some call for all-purpose flour, most use cake flour, which helps keep a cake tender when it is low in fat and sugar. Sifting the flour before measuring it was a standard technique at the time, and I have used it here in some cases, when it results in a better cake. If you don't have a sifter, you can press the flour through a strainer or remove and return to the container 1 tablespoon of the flour from each cup of unsifted flour after you have leveled it.

> "The mixer is more than a tool, it's a Friend; it will keep
> Your energy cost low
> Your success record high
> Your daughter on tiptoe to learn cakemaking"
> —*Woman's Home Companion*, October 1941

★ ★ ★ ★ ★ ★ "Cocoanut" Cake ★ ★ ★ ★ ★ ★ ★

In the 1940s coconut was often spelled with an a. This cake is quite different from the traditional white layers topped with sweet fluffy frosting and shredded fresh coconut that were familiar before the war. Although the availability of coconut must have been affected by the reassignment of merchant ships to military transport, coconut cakes appeared frequently in magazines and were promoted as "a taste of the tropics." This cake gets its sweetness from molasses, brown sugar, and the commercially sweetened coconut.

2 1/4 cups unsifted all-purpose flour
1 teaspoon baking powder
1/2 teaspoon baking soda
1/4 teaspoon salt
1/2 cup packed light brown sugar
1/4 cup vegetable shortening or
    softened butter (or a mixture)

1/2 cup light molasses
1 large egg
2/3 cup milk
1 cup sweetened shredded coconut
2 tablespoons confectioners' sugar

Preheat oven to 350°F. Generously grease a 9-inch square baking pan. Stir together flour, baking powder, soda, and salt in a small bowl.

Beat brown sugar and shortening in a large bowl with an electric mixer on high speed; gradually beat in molasses and egg. Add dry ingredients and milk to molasses mixture; beat on low speed until thoroughly blended. Fold in 3/4 cup coconut.

Transfer the batter to the greased pan; sprinkle with remaining 1/4 cup coconut and bake 35 to 40 minutes or until the center springs back when lightly pressed.

Cool cake in pan 15 minutes. Remove to serving plate and serve warm or cool completely. Dust with confectioners' sugar before serving.

8 Servings

★ ★ ★ ★ ★ ★ Creole Layer Cake ★ ★ ★ ★ ★ ★

In this case the name "Creole" was associated with the Caribbean Islands and the molasses and spices that they were known for before the war. The photograph of this cake in the November 1942 issue of Better Homes and Gardens *is captioned, "A dusky beauty, glamorous with spices." The use of dark corn syrup for a sweetener gives the cake a mellow, very mild molasses flavor that doesn't overwhelm the spices that provide its identity.*

2½ cups sifted cake flour (sift
   before measuring)
2 teaspoons baking powder
½ teaspoon salt
½ teaspoon ground cinnamon
¼ teaspoon baking soda
¼ teaspoon ground cloves
¼ teaspoon ground nutmeg

¾ cup packed light brown sugar
⅓ cup vegetable shortening or
   softened butter (or a mixture)
½ cup dark corn syrup
2 large eggs, beaten
1 cup buttermilk
Creole Frosting, recipe follows

Preheat oven to 350°F. Grease and flour two 9-inch round baking pans. Line bottoms with wax paper or parchment and grease again. Sift or stir together the flour, baking powder, salt, cinnamon, soda, cloves, and nutmeg.

Beat the brown sugar and shortening with an electric mixer on high speed until fluffy; gradually beat in the corn syrup and eggs. Add the dry ingredients alternately with the buttermilk and beat on low speed, scraping side of the bowl occasionally, just until smooth.

Divide the batter into the prepared pans and bake 25 to 30 minutes or until the centers spring back when lightly pressed.

Cool layers in pans 5 minutes. Remove to wire racks and cool completely. Fill and frost with Creole Frosting. Store in the refrigerator.

Creole Frosting: Combine 1 cup heavy cream, ¹/₂ teaspoon vanilla extract, ¹/₄ teaspoon ground cinnamon, and ¹/₈ teaspoon salt. Beat until stiff peaks form; beat in ¹/₄ cup dark corn syrup and 2 tablespoons confectioners' sugar.

10 Servings

"Good Eating depends on good cooking. Today—even more than ever before—good cooks appreciate good recipes. They want thoroughly tested interesting recipes they can count on for food that will be nourishing, appetizing, and readily digestible."—*Recipes for Good Eating,* 1945

★ ★ ★ ★ ★ ★ Ginger-Raisin Cake ★ ★ ★ ★ ★ ★

Molasses provides most of the sweetness and sour cream the richness in this quick spice cake. Frost it with Victory Frosting (page 44) for an unforbidden treat.

2¾ cups unsifted cake flour

1 tablespoon ground ginger

1 teaspoon ground cinnamon

1 teaspoon baking soda

½ teaspoon salt

1 cup light molasses

1 cup sour cream

¼ cup sugar

1 large egg

¾ cup dark seedless raisins

Preheat oven to 350°F. Generously grease two 9-inch round baking pans. Combine flour, ginger, cinnamon, soda, and salt in a sifter or stir together in a small bowl.

Stir together molasses, sour cream, sugar, and egg in a medium bowl with a spoon. Sift or spoon dry ingredients over molasses mixture and stir until thoroughly blended; fold in raisins. Transfer the batter to the prepared pans and bake 25 to 30 minutes or until the centers spring back when lightly pressed.

Cool cakes in pans 15 minutes. Remove to cooling rack and cool completely. Fill and frost with Victory Frosting (see page 44).

10 Servings

"Cakes were masterpieces then: beautiful to behold and marvelous to eat. Nearly everyone occasionally likes to turn back time, to live vicariously in a pattern before the present."—Jeanne M. Hall and Belle Anderson Ebner, *500 Recipes by Request: From Mother Anderson's Famous Dutch Kitchens,* 1948

★ ★ ★ ★ ★ ★ ★ **Harvest Cake** ★ ★ ★ ★ ★ ★ ★

Adapted from a 1943 cake flour advertisement, this recipe produces a spectacular three-layer cake using only ¹/₂ cup of shortening and a little added richness from the half-and-half. The original recipe suggested sifting the dry ingredients together three times before adding. This wasn't as time-consuming a task as it sounds. The ingredients could be measured directly into a special sifter that sifted through three screens at once. If you have a single-screen sifter you can sift just once; if you don't have a sifter, you can stir the dry ingredients together in a small bowl with a fork.

¹/₂ cup vegetable shortening or
    softened butter (or a mixture)

³/₄ cup sugar

2 large eggs, separated

2¹/₂ cups sifted cake flour (sift
    before measuring)

3 teaspoons baking powder

¹/₂ teaspoon salt

1 cup half-and-half

¹/₂ teaspoon vanilla extract

3 tablespoons chopped walnuts or
    pecans

1 tablespoon grated orange peel

¹/₄ teaspoon orange flavoring

Yellow food coloring

Preheat oven to 375°F. Grease and flour three 8-inch round baking pans.

Beat the shortening with an electric mixer on high speed until fluffy; gradually beat in ¹/₄ cup of the sugar. Beat in the egg yolks all at once. Combine the flour, baking powder, and salt in a sifter and sift over shortening mixture; add the half-and-half and beat on low speed, scraping side of bowl occasionally, just until smooth.

With clean beaters, beat the egg whites at high speed in a medium bowl until they are fluffy. Very gradually beat in the remaining ¹/₂ cup sugar until the mixture is stiff; fold the beaten whites into the batter just until no white streaks remain.

Remove one-third of the batter to a small bowl; stir in the vanilla and transfer to one of the prepared pans. Stir the nuts, orange peel, orange flavoring, and several drops food coloring into the remaining batter and divide between the 2 remaining prepared pans. Bake 20 to 25 minutes or until the centers spring back when lightly pressed.

Cool layers in pans 5 minutes. Remove to wire racks and cool completely before filling and frosting. Assemble with plain layer in the center.

10 Servings

★ ★ ★ ★ ★ ★ Hurry Scurry Cake ★ ★ ★ ★ ★ ★ ★

Speed is the theme in this two-step cake. Young home-front warriors can be enlisted to snip the marshmallows. Be sure to use large marshmallows—the minis were not available in the 1940s.

²/₃ cup sugar

¹/₃ cup vegetable shortening or
   softened butter (or a mixture)

1 large egg

1 teaspoon vanilla extract

¹/₄ teaspoon salt

1¹/₂ cups sifted cake flour
   (sift before measuring)

¹/₂ cup milk

1¹/₂ teaspoons baking powder

10 marshmallows, cut in half
   with a moistened scissors

Preheat oven to 350°F. Grease and flour an 8- by 2-inch round baking pan.

Combine sugar, shortening, egg, vanilla, and salt in a large bowl. Beat with an electric mixer on low speed until combined. Add flour, milk, and baking powder; increase speed to medium and beat 2 minutes, scraping side of bowl occasionally.

Transfer the batter to the prepared pan. Arrange marshmallows on top, cut side down, and bake 30 to 35 minutes or until a toothpick inserted between marshmallows in the center comes out clean.

Cool cake in pan 15 minutes before cutting. Cut into wedges and serve from pan.

6 to 8 Servings

"Sift flour just before using it. Then measure it, spooning it gently into the measuring cup. Using a spatula or knife, cut the excess flour off the top of the cup sharply."—*Down-On-The-Farm Cook Book,* 1943

★ ★ ★ ★ ★ ★ ★ ★ Jiffy Cake ★ ★ ★ ★ ★ ★ ★ ★

This quick cake can be served warm as the base for a cottage pudding or shortcake or cooled and frosted. Jiffy cakes appeared in most wartime cookbooks. They relied on a new one-bowl technique using an electric mixer and were publicized by electric mixer manufacturers. However, I found in testing this recipe that I got a more tender cake when I just stirred it together with a fork—and it was even easier.

1½ cups sifted cake flour
    (sift before measuring)
½ cup sugar
1½ teaspoons baking powder
¼ teaspoon salt

¾ cup milk
½ cup vegetable shortening or
    butter (or a mixture), melted
1 large egg, beaten
2 teaspoons vanilla extract

Preheat oven to 350°F. Grease and flour an 8-inch square baking pan. Combine flour, sugar, baking powder, and salt in a large bowl. Make a well in the center and add milk, shortening, egg, and vanilla. Beat with a fork until just combined—about 1 minute.

Pour the batter into the prepared pan and bake 25 to 30 minutes or until the center springs back when lightly pressed.

Cool in pan at least 5 minutes, then cut and serve warm with fruit topping. Or, remove to wire rack and cool completely, then frost.

9 Servings

"After the last war, eggs cost 92¢ a dozen, sugar 26¢ a pound. Let's make sure that the price control we have in this war continues to keep prices down!"
— War Information News Service bulletin, November 1944

★ ★ ★ ★ ★ LaFayette Gingerbread ★ ★ ★ ★ ★

Lafayette Gingerbread is well known in the South. It is reputed to be the cake served to Lafayette by George Washington's mother. The recipe was so famous by the 1940s that advertisements for a well-known gingerbread mix claimed on the label that it was "Washington's Mother's Own Recipe." The recipe that follows is adapted from one that appears in the community cookbook, "From North Carolina Kitchens: Favorite Recipes Old and New."

½ cup vegetable shortening or
   softened butter (or a mixture)

½ cup packed light brown sugar

1 cup dark molasses

3 large eggs

½ cup milk

½ cup orange juice

½ cup coffee or water

3 cups unsifted all-purpose flour

2 tablespoons ground ginger

2 tablespoons grated orange peel

2 teaspoons ground cinnamon

2 teaspoons ground mace

2 teaspoons ground nutmeg

1½ teaspoons baking soda

¼ teaspoon salt

1 cup dark seedless raisins

Preheat oven to 350°F. Grease and flour a 13- by 9-inch baking pan.

Beat the shortening and brown sugar in a large bowl with an electric mixer on high speed until fluffy; gradually beat in the molasses. Add the eggs one at a time, beating well after each addition. Beat in the milk, orange juice, and coffee one at a time. Then add the flour, ginger, orange peel, cinnamon, mace, nutmeg, soda, and salt all at once and beat on low speed just until smooth. Fold in the raisins.

Pour the batter into the prepared pan and bake 35 to 40 minutes or until the center springs back when lightly pressed.

Cool in pan 5 minutes. Cut into 12 rectangles and serve warm.

12 Servings

★ ★ ★ ★ ★ Mincemeat Fruit Cake ★ ★ ★ ★ ★

This recipe, from a 1943 community cookbook, uses a clever trick for getting the fruit, spice, and additional sweetness into the cake using mincemeat and apple butter that are most likely already available, home canned, on pantry shelves. These days both are available in the supermarket. The note accompanying it says that "it can be served at once or aged as for ordinary fruit cake."

2½ cups sifted cake flour (sift before measuring)

2 teaspoons baking powder

½ teaspoon salt

¼ teaspoon baking soda

¾ cup sugar

½ cup vegetable shortening or softened butter (or a mixture)

2 large eggs, beaten

2 teaspoons vanilla extract

1 pound mincemeat

½ cup apple butter

1 cup chopped nuts

Preheat oven to 325 °F. Grease a 10-inch tube pan; line bottom with wax paper or parchment and grease again. Sift or stir together the flour, baking powder, salt, and soda.

Beat the sugar and shortening with an electric mixer on high speed until fluffy; gradually beat in the eggs and vanilla. Add the dry ingredients; beat on low speed, scraping side of bowl occasionally, just until combined. Fold in mincemeat, apple butter, and nuts until thoroughly blended.

Transfer the mixture to the prepared pan and bake 60 to 65 minutes or until the top feels firm when lightly pressed.

Cool cake in pan 15 minutes. Remove to wire rack and cool completely.

Serve, or wrap in cheesecloth that has been soaked in brandy or other spirits, place in a tight container, and refrigerate until ready to serve.

10 Servings

★ ★ ★ Molasses Bread Crumb Cake ★ ★ ★

This thrifty 1944 recipe certainly meets all the wartime guidelines. It uses very little shortening and sugar, incorporates nutritious whole wheat flour and molasses, can be assembled quickly, and even makes use of some day-old bread crumbs. This was originally topped with unbaked meringue, but Victory Frosting (page 44) is a safer option these days because the egg whites have been heated, and it provides a similar flavor. The corn flake topping is a creative wartime substitute for nuts.

1 cup whole wheat flour

1/4 cup sugar

2 teaspoons ginger

3/4 teaspoon baking soda

1/2 teaspoon salt

1/2 cup boiling water

1/4 cup vegetable shortening or
   butter (or a mixture)

1/2 cup light molasses

1 large egg

1 cup day-old bread crumbs

3/4 cup dark seedless raisins

1/2 recipe Victory Frosting (page 44)

1/2 cup corn flakes

2 tablespoons coarsely chopped
   candied cherries

Preheat oven to 350°F. Generously grease an 8-inch square baking pan. Stir together flour, sugar, ginger, soda, and salt in a small bowl.

Pour boiling water over shortening in a large bowl; gradually beat in molasses and egg with a rotary beater or a whisk. Fold dry ingredients, crumbs, and raisins into molasses mixture until thoroughly blended.

Transfer the batter to the greased pan and bake 35 to 40 minutes or until the center springs back when lightly pressed.

Cool cake in pan 15 minutes. Invert onto serving plate and cool completely. Frost top with Victory Frosting (see page 44), allowing it to drip down the side slightly. Sprinkle with corn flakes and cherries.

8 Servings

★ ★ ★ ★ ★ ★ Raisin Fruitcake ★ ★ ★ ★ ★ ★

This simple fruitcake appeared in a December 1943 cake flour advertisement as a "Holiday Double Feature." Homemakers were told, "In a time of shortages, you daydream of a recipe like this!…Few eggs, little sugar, little shortening—but you still get moist, mellow, rich-tasting cake…." They were advised to frost one loaf or top it with nuts for their holiday use and to leave the other one plain so it could be packed to "send away." Seeded raisins are not easy to find these days, but dark seedless ones may be substituted.

4 cups seeded raisins

2¼ cups cold, strong coffee

2 tablespoons grated lemon or
    orange peel

1 tablespoon ground cinnamon

1 teaspoon ground allspice

2 cups walnuts, pecans or hazelnuts

4 cups sifted cake flour (sift before
    measuring)

1½ cups sugar

5 teaspoons baking powder

2 teaspoons salt

½ cup vegetable shortening or
    softened butter (or a mixture)

2 large eggs, beaten

2 teaspoons vanilla extract

Frosting or jam and chopped nuts,
    optional

Combine raisins, coffee, lemon peel, cinnamon, and allspice in a medium saucepan; bring to a boil over high heat. Reduce heat to low, cover and simmer 8 minutes. Pour mixture into a colander or strainer over a bowl, catching liquid in a large measuring cup. Press raisins to release as much moisture as possible. Add additional coffee to measured liquid to make 1½ cups; set aside. Grind raisins and nuts in a grinder or finely chop in food processor.

Meanwhile, grease two 9-inch loaf pans; line with parchment or aluminum foil and grease again. Stir together flour, sugar, baking powder, and salt in a medium bowl. Preheat oven to 350 °F.

Beat shortening in a large bowl; beat in eggs and vanilla. Add dry ingredients, and reserved liquid; beat just until thoroughly blended. Fold in raisin mixture. Divide batter between prepared loaf pans.

Bake 55 to 60 minutes or until a toothpick inserted in the center comes out clean.

Cool to room temperature and serve or pack in an airtight container.

Frost or spread with jam and top with nuts, if desired.

16 Servings

★ ★ ★ ★ ★ Red Devil's Food Cake ★ ★ ★ ★ ★

The method for this cake was billed as "Mix-Easy" to meet the needs of the increasing number of working mothers who had very little time for baking, yet felt that it was a part of their patriotic duty to serve a complete meal, including dessert, every evening. It is good topped with a half-recipe of Peanut Butter–Condensed Milk Frosting (page 43) and shaved chocolate or a half-recipe of Victory Frosting (page 44) and crushed candy canes. I was surprised that the Red Devil's Food Cake recipes I found in wartime cookbooks did not include red food coloring as is sometimes done today. The name comes from the fact that the interaction of cocoa and baking soda produces a beautiful reddish-brown cake without adding color. The earliest recipe I have found that includes artificial color was published in the mid-1960s.

1½ cups sifted cake flour
   (sift before measuring)

1 cup sugar

¾ teaspoon baking soda

½ teaspoon salt

¾ cup boiling water

2 (1-ounce) squares unsweetened
   chocolate, chopped

½ cup vegetable shortening or
   softened butter (or a mixture)

2 large eggs

2 teaspoons vanilla extract

Preheat oven to 350°F. Grease and flour an 8-inch square baking pan. Combine flour, sugar, soda, and salt in a sifter. Stir together water and chocolate in a small bowl until chocolate has melted; set aside.

Beat the shortening in a large bowl with an electric mixer on high speed until fluffy; beat in eggs and vanilla all at once. Sift the dry ingredients over the shortening mixture. Add the chocolate mixture; beat on low speed just until smooth.

Transfer the batter to the prepared pan and bake 30 to 35 minutes or until the center springs back when lightly pressed.

Cool cake in pan 5 minutes. Remove to wire racks and cool completely before frosting.

9 Servings

★ ★ ★ ★ ★ ★ ★ Service Cake ★ ★ ★ ★ ★ ★ ★ ★

Based on a recipe from a Betty Crocker pamphlet called "Your Share," this versatile cake "serves" as the basis for other desserts. It can be enjoyed plain as a "farm" cake, frosted with a half recipe of frosting; as a cottage pudding with a fruit or chocolate sauce; or baked with a crumb, coconut, or nut topping.

1¹/₃ cups unsifted all-purpose flour

1¹/₂ teaspoons baking powder

¹/₂ teaspoon salt

²/₃ cup sugar

¹/₃ cup vegetable shortening or
   softened butter (or a mixture)

2 large eggs

¹/₂ cup milk

1¹/₂ teaspoons vanilla extract

Preheat oven to 350°F. Grease an 8- by 2-inch round baking pan. Sift or stir together the flour, baking powder, and salt.

Beat the sugar and shortening with an electric mixer on high speed until fluffy; beat in the eggs all at once. Add the dry ingredients, milk, and vanilla; beat on low speed, scraping side of bowl occasionally, just until smooth.

Transfer the batter to the greased pan and bake 30 to 35 minutes or until the center springs back when lightly pressed.

Cool in pan 5 minutes. Remove to wire rack and cool at least 15 minutes before serving warm, or cool completely to frost.

8 Servings

★ ★ ★ ★ Sugarless Chocolate Cake ★ ★ ★ ★

The meringue method, in which corn syrup is gradually beaten into egg whites, not only makes it possible to produce a tender cake using no granulated sugar, but it increases the volume of the layers in comparison to those made with granulated sugar and unbeaten eggs. This recipe can be used to make yellow cake layers by eliminating the chocolate and adding ¼ cup sifted cake flour. In this recipe it is very important to use cake flour, not all-purpose flour, and to sift it so that it is not packed in the cup.

2¾ cups sifted cake flour
   (sift before measuring)

3 teaspoons baking powder

½ teaspoon salt

½ cup vegetable shortening or
   softened butter (or a mixture)

1½ cups light corn syrup

3 large eggs, separated

¾ cup milk

4 (1-ounce) squares semisweet
   chocolate, melted

2 teaspoons vanilla extract

Preheat oven to 350°F. Grease two 9-inch round baking pans and line with waxed paper or parchment; grease paper. Stir together flour, baking powder, and salt.

Beat the shortening with an electric mixer on high speed until fluffy; gradually beat in ¾ cup of the corn syrup. Beat in the egg yolks all at once. Add the dry ingredients, milk, chocolate, and vanilla; beat on low speed just until smooth.

With clean beaters, beat the egg whites at high speed in a medium bowl until they are fluffy. Very gradually beat in the remaining ¾ cup corn syrup until the mixture is stiff; fold the beaten whites into the chocolate batter just until no white streaks remain.

Divide the batter into the prepared pans and bake 25 to 30 minutes or until the centers spring back when lightly pressed.

Cool layers in pans 5 minutes. Remove to wire racks and cool completely before filling and frosting.

10 Servings

★ ★ ★ ★ Sweet Potato Victory Cake ★ ★ ★ ★

Light on both sugar and butter, this easy one-bowl cake was a perfect solution to the problem of providing a sweet dessert during World War II. It could be assembled quickly by a busy home-front cook, and chances are the sweet potatoes came from a backyard Victory Garden.

1 cup mashed sweet potatoes, warm

²/₃ cup sugar

¹/₄ cup vegetable shortening or
   softened butter (or a mixture)

3 tablespoons lemon juice

1 teaspoon cinnamon

¹/₂ teaspoon salt

¹/₄ teaspoon nutmeg

2 large eggs

1¹/₂ cups unsifted all-purpose flour

2 teaspoons baking powder

Confectioners' sugar or half recipe
   of frosting (see pages 41 to 44)

Preheat oven to 350°F. Grease and flour a 9-inch square baking pan. Beat the sweet potatoes, sugar, shortening, lemon juice, cinnamon, salt, and nutmeg in a large bowl with an electric mixer on high speed until fluffy. Add the eggs one at a time, beating well after each addition. Sprinkle the flour and baking powder over the mixture and beat on low speed, scraping side of bowl occasionally, just until smooth.

Pour the batter into the prepared pan and bake 30 to 35 minutes or until the center springs back when lightly pressed.

Cool cake in pan at least 5 minutes before cutting into 9 squares. Serve warm sprinkled with confectioners' sugar, or at room temperature topped with frosting. Store any leftovers in the refrigerator.

9 Servings

★ ★ ★ ★ ★ Three-Way Cake ★ ★ ★ ★ ★ ★

With just slightly reduced sugar and shortening, this basic yellow cake fit the bill during the early 1940s because it could be quickly and easily assembled when a celebration was in order. In an era before the widespread availability of cake mixes, the advertised reliability of the recipe gave novice bakers the confidence to give it a try. The name came from the advertisement's suggestion that the batter be divided into a small round pan, 6 cupcake pans, and a small loaf pan to make three different dessert presentations for three wartime dinners.

3 cups sifted cake flour (sift before measuring)

3 teaspoons baking powder

½ teaspoon salt

⅔ cup vegetable shortening or softened butter (or a mixture)

1 cup sugar

3 large eggs

1 cup milk

3 teaspoons vanilla extract

Preheat oven to 350°F. Grease and flour three 8-inch round baking pans (or 1 round, 1 loaf, and 6 cupcake pans.) Sift or stir together the flour, baking powder, and salt.

Beat the shortening with an electric mixer on high speed until fluffy; gradually beat in the sugar. Add the eggs one at a time, beating well after each addition. Add the dry ingredients, milk, and vanilla; beat on low speed, scraping side of bowl occasionally, just until smooth.

Divide the batter into the prepared pans and bake layers 25 to 30 minutes or until the centers spring back when lightly pressed. (A 7-inch loaf cake should take about 35 minutes and cupcakes 18 to 20.)

Cool cakes in pans 5 minutes. Remove to wire racks and cool completely before filling, if necessary, and frosting.

18 Servings

★ ★ ★ ★ ★ ★ ★ ★ War Cake ★ ★ ★ ★ ★ ★ ★ ★

The name War Cake was used for several different cakes. All are sweetened by honey or molasses and are served with only a dusting of confectioners' sugar. This is the quickest version to prepare.

2 cups sifted cake flour
  (sift before measuring)
2 teaspoons baking powder
¼ teaspoon salt
⅔ cup vegetable shortening or
  softened butter (or a mixture)

1 cup honey
3 large eggs
1 teaspoon vanilla extract
Confectioners' sugar, optional

Preheat oven to 325°F. Grease and flour an 8-inch square baking pan. Combine flour, baking powder, and salt in a small bowl.

Beat shortening in a large bowl with an electric mixer on high speed; gradually beat in honey, eggs, and vanilla. Add dry ingredients; beat with an electric mixer on low speed until combined.

Transfer batter to prepared pan. Bake until golden and a toothpick inserted in center comes out clean, 55 to 60 minutes. Cool 10 minutes in pan. Cut into rectangles and serve warm with a dusting of confectioners' sugar, if desired.

6 to 8 Servings

"Cakes are the cook's triumph. It takes skill, patience, and practice to turn out a perfect cake, but there is no other product so satisfying."—*The New Hood Cook Book*, 1941

★ ★ ★ ★ ★ ★ ★ Wedding Cake ★ ★ ★ ★ ★ ★ ★ ★

A part of every family cookbook since the early nineteenth century, this 1-2-3-4 cake recipe was only used for a very special occasion during rationing. Wartime memoirs tell of the whole family contributing ration coupons in order to get the sugar for a wedding cake. Weddings were often small and quickly planned to coincide with a serviceman's furlough. The cake was definitely the centerpiece of the wedding reception, and was often the only food served, accompanied by a bowl of punch.

2 cups sugar	3 teaspoons baking powder
1 cup (2 sticks) butter, softened	½ teaspoon salt
4 large eggs, separated	1 cup milk
3 cups sifted cake flour (sift before measuring)	2 teaspoons vanilla extract
	Desired frosting (pages 41 to 44)

Preheat oven to 350°F. Grease and flour three 9-inch round baking pans.

Beat the sugar and butter in a large bowl with an electric mixer on high speed until fluffy; gradually beat in the egg yolks. Combine the flour, baking powder, and salt in a sifter or sieve; sift over the sugar mixture; then add milk and vanilla and beat on low speed just until smooth.

With clean beaters, beat the egg whites until soft peaks form; fold beaten whites into batter and divide into the prepared pans.

Bake 25 to 30 minutes or until the centers spring back when lightly pressed.

Cool layers in pans 5 minutes. Remove to wire racks and cool completely before filling and frosting.

12 Servings

WARTIME SPECIAL

Blueberry-Honey Cake

Although I remember my grandmother making her sugar cookies with chicken fat, and have frequently seen it listed as an alternate for butter in recipes, very few recipes were published that actually called for chicken fat. Since it was usually made at home, it was not in short supply. This recipe is based on one from the February 1943 issue of Farm Journal and Farmer's Wife *that also uses honey and home-canned berries or cherries. Serve this cake with colorful lemonade that has been sweetened with the syrup from the jar of fruit and you are truly a home-front hero.*

2 ¾ cups unsifted all-purpose flour
3 teaspoons baking powder
1 teaspoon ground cinnamon
½ teaspoon baking soda
½ teaspoon salt
¼ teaspoon ground nutmeg
1 cup honey

⅔ cup chicken fat (or butter), softened
2 large eggs
⅔ cup milk
1 cup drained canned blueberries, blackberries, or cherries
Penuche Frosting (recipe follows)

Preheat oven to 375°F. Grease and flour three 9-inch round baking pans. Stir together the flour, baking powder, cinnamon, soda, salt, and nutmeg in a medium bowl.

Beat the honey and chicken fat or butter with an electric mixer on high speed until fluffy; beat in the eggs all at once. Spoon the dry ingredients over the honey mixture; add the milk and beat on low speed, scraping side of bowl occasionally, just until smooth. Fold in the berries.

Divide the batter among the prepared pans and bake 20 to 25 minutes or until the centers spring back when lightly pressed.

Cool layers in pans 5 minutes. Remove to wire racks and cool completely. Fill between layers and frost just the top with Frosting.

Penuche Frosting: Combine **2 cups packed light brown sugar, 1/2 cup milk, 1/4 cup shortening or butter,** and **2 tablespoons light corn syrup** in a heavy saucepan. Bring to a boil and cook to 220°F, stirring constantly, about 1 minute. Remove from heat. Stir in **1/2 teaspoon vanilla extract** and beat until thick and spreadable.

10 Servings

"Butter is preferable to any other shortening, but if the food allowance does not permit the use of butter, then a vegetable shortening should be used. One good plan is to use half-and-half, butter and vegetable shortening. In this manner the good flavor of the butter in the cake is secured."—*Army Mess Management Simplified,* 1942

★ ★ ★ ★ They Also Served ★ ★ ★ ★

SMALL CAKES, FROSTINGS, AND FILLINGS

Apple Coffee Cake

Boston Cream Pie

Jelly Roll

Nut Cupcakes

One-Egg Cupcakes

Orange Pour Cake

Peanut Butter–Chocolate Cupcakes

Pineapple Upside-Down Cake

Prune Nut Cake

Quick Spice Cupcakes

Cocoa Cream Frosting

Maple-Marshmallow Frosting

Peanut Butter–Condensed Milk Frosting

Victory Frosting

Fillings

WARTIME SPECIAL

Melody Mélange

"Save your 'blue' stamps by using Fresh Fruits in season when abundant and at their best—by extending canned Fruits—by using dried Fruits for variety."—*Your Share*, 1943

IN A SECTION ENTITLED "You can have your cake and eat it, too" Betty Crocker's pamphlet *Your Share: How to prepare appetizing, healthful meals with foods available today* suggests that homemakers "Make smaller cakes. Use ¹/₂ or ¹/₃ of recipe. Make cup cakes." In another section it suggests that coffee cakes and sweet rolls make good desserts because they use less sugar than regular cakes. This chapter includes cakes that fit into those categories and a selection of wartime frostings and "sugarless" fillings that can be used on the cakes in Chapter One as well.

World War II homemakers were encouraged to always serve a complete meal including dessert, and these small cakes filled that spot and provided sweetness with a minimum of fuss. Cupcakes were especially useful for the wartime baker because they are portion-controlled and travel well in packed lunches. They can be frosted or not, retain their moistness better than a piece of cake that has a cut surface, and can even be wrapped individually and shipped to family in the service. Although smaller in size than today's cupcakes, top them with any of the frostings or fillings in this chapter and you have a serving of cake worthy of any celebration. Always placed first in the frosting section of 1940s cookbooks, fluffy, egg white–based frostings were clearly the favorite choice in the home-front kitchen. They could be made with corn syrup, honey, maple syrup, brown sugar, or almost any sweet you had on hand, produced a lot of frosting with just a few ingredients, were easy to apply, and looked spectacular. Although they appear less frequently today because of our concern for egg safety, they still have all those convenient characteristics when heated sufficiently (see Victory Frosting, page 44).

"Frost your cake and have your sugar, too! Omit icing on sides of layer cakes . . . loaf cakes require less icing than layer cakes. Layer cakes with fillings take less icing."—*Your Share*, 1943

★ ★ ★ ★ ★ Apple Coffee Cake ★ ★ ★ ★ ★ ★

Apple Cake was a World War II favorite, but many of the cakes had the apples on top of the cake and it was difficult to get them tender. In this cake they bake to perfection under the batter, making a generous apple topping when the cake is inverted.

4 large cooking apples, peeled and
  sliced

⅓ cup packed light brown sugar

2 tablespoons margarine or butter
  (or a mixture), melted

¼ teaspoon ground nutmeg

⅛ teaspoon ground allspice

1½ cups sifted cake flour (sift before
  measuring)

3 tablespoons granulated sugar

3 teaspoons baking powder

¼ teaspoon salt

¼ cup vegetable shortening or
  softened butter (or a mixture)

1 large egg

½ cup milk

Preheat oven to 350°F. Grease a 9-inch square baking dish. Combine apples, brown sugar, margarine, nutmeg, and allspice in baking dish. Combine flour, granulated sugar, baking powder, and salt in a small bowl.

Beat shortening and egg in a medium bowl with an electric mixer on high speed until combined; beat in milk. Add dry ingredients and beat on low speed just until combined. Spread batter over apples.

Bake until cake springs back when gently pressed, 35 to 40 minutes. Cool cake in pan 5 minutes; loosen edges and invert onto serving plate. Cut into squares and serve warm.

6 Servings

★ ★ ★ ★ ★ ★ Boston Cream Pie ★ ★ ★ ★ ★ ★ ★

The layer of hot-milk sponge cake in this recipe creates a special dessert without using much fat. However, the amount of sugar used in this recipe, although reduced from the conventional version, did put it in the category of occasional treats during the war. You can also fill and top the split layer with strawberries and cream for Strawberry Shortcake, or fill the layer with jam and sprinkle confectioners' sugar over the top for Washington Pie.

$1/4$ cup milk

1 tablespoon vegetable shortening or butter (or a mixture)

$1/3$ cup sifted all-purpose flour (sift before measuring)

$3/4$ teaspoon baking powder

$1/4$ teaspoon salt

2 large eggs

$2/3$ cup sugar

3 teaspoons vanilla extract

Custard Filling, recipe follows

$1/2$ cup Cocoa Cream Frosting (page 41)

Preheat oven to 350°F. Grease and flour a deep 8-inch round baking pan.

Heat milk and shortening in a small saucepan over very low heat until shortening melts and bubbles start to appear at the edge of the pan, 3 to 5 minutes. Sift or stir together the flour, baking powder, and salt.

Beat the eggs with an electric mixer on high speed until thick and light; very gradually beat in the sugar. Fold in the dry ingredients until thoroughly blended. Add the vanilla, then very gradually whisk in the hot milk mixture.

Pour the batter into the prepared pan and bake 25 to 30 minutes or until the center springs back when lightly pressed. Meanwhile, prepare custard filling, cool.

Cool cake layer in pan 5 minutes. Remove to serving plate and split crosswise.

Spoon Custard Filling onto bottom half of layer; add top of cake layer and frost with Cocoa Cream Frosting. Serve immediately or refrigerate until ready to serve. Store any leftovers in refrigerator.

Custard Filling: Combine **2 tablespoons all-purpose flour**, **1 tablespoon sugar**, and **⅛ teaspoon salt** in a small, heavy, saucepan. Stir in **1 cup milk** until smooth. Cook over very low heat, stirring constantly, until thickened, 6 to 8 minutes. Gradually beat about one-third of the mixture into **1 egg yolk** in a small bowl until thoroughly blended; gradually beat yolk mixture into remaining milk mixture in saucepan. Return just to a boil, stirring constantly; remove from heat and stir in ½ **teaspoon vanilla extract**.

8 to 10 Servings

FOOD IS A WEAPON

DON'T WASTE IT !
BUY WISELY - COOK CAREFULLY - EAT IT ALL

"On Monday morning after Sunday's bombing in Hawaii, apparently the first war action that many women took was going to the store for sugar. Eager purchasers knew . . . there would be a shortage, not only because sugar had to be shipped over now-perilous seas, but also because industry would soon compete with housewives for the precious sweet stuff."—*American Women and World War II,* 1990

★ ★ ★ ★ ★ ★ ★ ★ ★ Jelly Roll ★ ★ ★ ★ ★ ★ ★ ★ ★

A 1944 vegetable shortening advertisement claimed that their product produced lighter cakes without even creaming the shortening to soften it. To prove it they offered this recipe, which beats the shortening with the dry ingredients and half of the eggs using an electric mixer. The results live up to the advertisement.

1 cup sifted cake flour
   (sift before measuring)

1 cup sugar

1½ teaspoons baking powder

¼ teaspoon salt

½ cup vegetable shortening or
   softened butter (or a mixture)

4 large eggs

2 teaspoons vanilla extract

¼ cup confectioners' sugar

1 cup seedless red raspberry or
   apricot jam

Preheat oven to 375°F. Grease a jelly roll pan; line with parchment or waxed paper and grease paper.

Stir together the flour, sugar, baking powder, and salt in a large bowl. Add the shortening, 2 eggs, and the vanilla to the dry ingredients and beat with an electric mixer on high speed until fluffy. Separate the remaining 2 eggs. Place the whites in a small bowl and beat the yolks into the batter.

With clean beaters, beat the egg whites at high speed until they are stiff; fold beaten whites into the batter just until no white streaks remain. Spread batter into the prepared pan and bake until the center springs back when lightly pressed, about 15 minutes.

Sift confectioners' sugar over a linen towel that has been spread out on a work surface; invert cake onto towel and remove paper. Trim off crisp edges; spread cake with jam and roll up.

Roll cake in towel and set aside, open side down, until completely cool, about 30 minutes. Transfer to serving plate and slice crosswise.

8 Servings

★ ★ ★ ★ ★ ★ ★ Nut Cupcakes ★ ★ ★ ★ ★ ★ ★

Locally produced nuts were a big help to wartime bakers, because the normal transportation systems that brought walnuts and almonds from California and pecans from Texas and Georgia were tied up carrying essential war materials. Recipes like this one that call for whatever nut you can get were the norm.

1 cup sifted cake flour
  (sift before measuring)
1½ teaspoons baking powder
¼ teaspoon salt
½ cup packed light brown sugar
⅓ cup vegetable shortening or
  softened butter (or a mixture)

1 large egg
½ cup milk
2 teaspoons vanilla extract
¾ cup finely chopped walnuts,
  pecans, hazelnuts, or almonds
Confectioners' sugar or frosting

Preheat oven to 350°F. Grease and flour a 12-cup muffin pan. Sift or stir together the flour, baking powder, and salt.

Beat the brown sugar and shortening with an electric mixer on high speed until fluffy; beat in the egg. Add the dry ingredients, milk, and vanilla; beat on low speed just until smooth. Fold in the nuts.

Divide the batter among the prepared cups and bake 18 to 20 minutes or until the centers spring back when lightly pressed.

Cool cupcakes in pans 5 minutes.

Remove to a wire rack and cool completely before dusting with confectioners' sugar or spreading with frosting.

12 Servings

★ ★ ★ ★ ★ ★ One-Egg Cupcakes ★ ★ ★ ★ ★ ★ ★

Cupcakes were (and still are) a good, quick dessert to make for lunch boxes and busy-day suppers. This recipe is so easy, it is a good first cake for young bakers.

1¼ cups unsifted all-purpose flour

2 teaspoons baking powder

¼ teaspoon salt

½ cup sugar

¼ cup vegetable shortening or
  softened butter (or a mixture)

½ cup milk

1 large egg

1 teaspoon vanilla extract

½ recipe frosting, optional
  (pages 41 to 44)

Heat oven to 375°F. Grease a 12-cup muffin pan. Combine flour, baking powder, and salt in a small bowl; set aside.

Beat sugar and shortening in a medium bowl until light and fluffy. Beat in milk, egg, and vanilla. Add the dry ingredients and stir just until they have been moistened. Do not overbeat.

Divide batter into greased muffin cups and bake 20 to 25 minutes or until a toothpick inserted in the center of one comes out clean.

Cool in pan 5 minutes. Remove to wire rack and frost, if desired.

12 Servings

 "In separating eggs, even the experts get a speck of yolk in with the whites from time to time. When that happens they just touch the yolk with a cloth moistened in cold water. The yolk speck will stick to the cloth and all will be well."—*Better Homes & Gardens*, December 1943

★ ★ ★ ★ ★ ★ Orange Pour Cake ★ ★ ★ ★ ★ ★ ★

The orange syrup that's poured over this cake after it is baked keeps it moist, and eliminates the need for frosting.

1²/₃ cups unsifted all-purpose flour	2 large eggs
1 teaspoon baking soda	³/₄ cup sour cream
¹/₂ teaspoon salt	3 teaspoons grated orange peel
¹/₂ cup vegetable shortening or softened butter (or a mixture)	¹/₄ cup granulated sugar
	¹/₄ cup orange juice
¹/₂ cup packed light brown sugar	

Preheat oven to 375°F. Grease a 9-inch square baking pan. Sift or stir together the flour, soda, and salt.

Beat the shortening and sugar with an electric mixer on high speed until fluffy; beat in the eggs all at once. Add the dry ingredients, sour cream, and 2 teaspoons orange peel; beat on low speed, scraping side of bowl occasionally, just until smooth.

Transfer the batter to the prepared pan and bake 25 to 30 minutes or until the center springs back when lightly pressed.

Remove pan to cooling rack.

Combine the granulated sugar, orange juice, and remaining 1 teaspoon orange peel in a small saucepan; heat until sugar dissolves. Drizzle over baked cake and set aside to cool completely before cutting into 9 squares.

9 Servings

★ ★ Peanut Butter–Chocolate Cupcakes ★ ★

This eggless chocolate batter gets most of its richness from peanut butter. It is essential that you use sifted cake flour rather than all-purpose flour, or the cupcakes will be less tender.

1³/₄ cup sifted cake flour
   (sift before measuring)

1 cup sugar

³/₄ teaspoon baking soda

¹/₂ teaspoon salt

¹/₄ cup peanut butter

2 tablespoons vegetable shortening
   or softened butter (or a mixture)

2 (1-ounce) squares unsweetened
   chocolate, melted

1 cup milk

2 teaspoons vanilla extract

Preheat oven to 350°F. Grease and flour a 12-cup muffin pan. Sift or stir together the flour, sugar, baking soda, and salt.

Beat the peanut butter, shortening, and chocolate with an electric mixer on high speed until fluffy. Add the dry ingredients, milk, and vanilla; beat on low speed, scraping side of bowl occasionally, until combined. Beat on high speed 30 seconds.

Divide the batter into the prepared pans and bake 20 to 25 minutes or until the centers spring back when lightly pressed.

Cool cupcakes in pans 5 minutes. Remove to wire racks and cool completely before frosting.

12 Servings

"To bake good things—put good things into them! . . . You can't get light, tender textures and delicate flavors with inferior ingredients."—*All About Home Baking*, 1937

★ ★ ★ Pineapple Upside-Down Cake ★ ★ ★

A 1943 Dole Hawaiian Pineapple Products advertisement advised homemakers, "If you don't find Dole Sliced Hawaiian Pineapple at your grocer's today, ask again tomorrow. Your blue stamps entitle you to your share of Hawaiian Pineapple Products after the Armed Forces are taken care of."

1 cup unsifted all-purpose flour

1½ teaspoons baking powder

¼ teaspoon salt

2 tablespoons butter or margarine, melted

½ cup packed light brown sugar

1 (8¼-ounce) can pineapple slices in heavy syrup

5 maraschino cherries or walnut halves

⅓ cup vegetable shortening or softened butter (or a mixture)

⅓ cup granulated sugar

1 large egg

2 teaspoons vanilla extract

Preheat oven to 350°F. Grease an 8-inch square baking pan. Sift or stir together the flour, baking powder, and salt.

Drizzle butter over bottom of pan and sprinkle with brown sugar. Drain pineapple slices, reserving ½ cup syrup (add water if necessary to make ½ cup). Arrange pineapple slices in pan. Place a cherry in the center of each pineapple slice and place fifth cherry in center of cake.

Beat the shortening with an electric mixer on high speed until fluffy; gradually beat in granulated sugar and egg. Add the dry ingredients, reserved pineapple syrup, and vanilla; beat on low speed, scraping side of bowl occasionally, just until smooth.

Spoon batter over pineapple in the prepared pan and bake 45 to 50 minutes or until the center springs back when lightly pressed.

Let stand 5 minutes, then loosen sides and invert onto serving plate. Serve warm.

8 Servings

★ ★ ★ ★ ★ ★ Prune Nut Cake ★ ★ ★ ★ ★ ★

Prune cakes were very popular during the war because they used little sugar, stayed moist, and shipped well. They became family favorites, and many different prune cake recipes appeared in community cookbooks well into the 1960s. Prunes have a less-than-glamorous image these days, but this recipe reminds us of what we're missing.

1¼ cups unsifted all-purpose flour

1¼ teaspoons baking powder

1 teaspoon ground cinnamon

¼ teaspoon baking soda

¼ teaspoon salt

½ cup sugar

¼ cup vegetable shortening or softened butter (or a mixture)

½ cup sour cream

2 large eggs, beaten

1 teaspoon vanilla extract

12 cooked sweetened prunes, well drained and quartered (½ cup), see Note

½ cup chopped nuts

Preheat oven to 350°F. Grease a 9-inch loaf pan. Combine flour, baking powder, cinnamon, soda, and salt in a small bowl. Beat sugar and shortening until fluffy. Beat in sour cream, eggs, and vanilla. Add dry ingredients and beat just until combined. Do not beat until smooth. Fold in prunes and nuts. Transfer batter to greased loaf pan.

Bake 45 to 50 minutes or until a toothpick inserted in the center comes out clean.

Cool to room temperature and serve or pack in an airtight container.

NOTE: You can buy cooked prunes in heavy syrup in a jar or simmer very large dried ones in lightly sweetened water until they are tender, about 8 minutes.

12 Servings

★ ★ ★ ★ ★ Quick Spice Cupcakes ★ ★ ★ ★ ★

You can have these easy, one-bowl cupcakes in the oven in fewer than five minutes. To make them even faster use 1½ teaspoons of apple pie or pumpkin pie spice in place of the individual spices.

½ cup sugar

1 large egg

⅓ cup vegetable shortening or
softened butter (or a mixture)

1 teaspoon vanilla extract

1¼ cups unsifted cake flour

1½ teaspoons baking powder

1 teaspoon ground cinnamon

¼ teaspoon ground cloves

¼ teaspoon ground nutmeg

¼ teaspoon salt

½ cup milk

¼ cup chopped walnuts

2 tablespoons confectioners' sugar

Preheat oven to 375°F. Grease 10 muffin pan cups or line with paper baking cups.

Combine the sugar, egg, shortening, and vanilla in a medium bowl. Beat with an electric mixer on high speed until thoroughly blended. Add the flour, baking powder, cinnamon, cloves, nutmeg, and salt directly into the bowl as you measure them. Add the milk and beat on low speed just until smooth.

Divide the batter into the greased muffin cups; top with walnuts. Bake 20 to 25 minutes or until the centers spring back when lightly pressed.

Cool cupcakes on wire racks at least 15 minutes. Sift confectioners' sugar over top and serve warm or at room temperature.

10 Servings

★ ★ ★ ★ ★ Cocoa Cream Frosting ★ ★ ★ ★ ★

You'll recognize this delicious old-fashioned cocoa frosting by the crisp, shiny surface and creamy texture that results when the shortening and sugar, slightly melted by the hot cream, firm up as they cool.

2 tablespoons vegetable shortening	2¼ cups unsifted confectioners' sugar
1 tablespoon butter	½ cup unsweetened cocoa powder
2 teaspoons vanilla extract	5 to 7 tablespoons heavy cream, heated
¼ teaspoon salt	

Beat shortening, butter, vanilla, and salt in a medium bowl with an electric beater until fluffy.

Combine confectioners' sugar and cocoa in a sifter or strainer and sift half of the mixture over the shortening mixture. Add 3 tablespoons cream and beat until combined.

Beat in remaining sugar mixture and as much of remaining cream as necessary to make a creamy, spreadable frosting. Use while still warm to fill and frost a 2-layer cake.

Frosts and fills a 9-inch 2-layer cake

 A March 1942 *Ladies' Home Journal* survey asked servicemen, "What is Your Dream Girl Like?" The results showed that the "Domestic type, fond of cooking and children" came out first and that "Business ability and braininess run a mighty poor second to a talent for cooking."

★ ★ ★ Maple-Marshmallow Frosting ★ ★ ★

Using a combination of available and unrationed ingredients, this easy frosting delivers maximum sweetness to the cakes it tops. It is best used on single-layer cakes that will be served from the pan, or on cupcakes so that it can drip onto wax paper before being transferred to a serving platter.

½ cup maple syrup

2 ounces large marshmallows,
  quartered

½ cup chopped nuts

Bring maple syrup to a boil in a medium saucepan over low heat. Allow to simmer 3 minutes. Stir in marshmallows; cook, stirring constantly, until marshmallows are almost melted. Pour over a 13- by 9-inch sheet cake or 12 cupcakes and sprinkle with nuts.

12 Servings

"It is not necessary for the Army cook to be able to make a wide variety of cakes, but each time he bakes he should endeavor to improve the quality and texture of his product, so that in time he may learn to bake a cake of which he may be truly proud."—*Army Mess Management Simplified*, 1942

★ ★ ★ ★ ★ ★ Peanut Butter– ★ ★ ★ ★ ★ ★ Condensed Milk Frosting

Sweetened condensed milk usually counts on the acid in whatever is added to it to cause it to thicken. In this case it is heat that will do it, so you have to be patient, but you will be rewarded with the world's easiest peanut butter frosting.

1 (14-ounce) can sweetened
  condensed milk

3 tablespoons smooth peanut butter

Combine sweetened condensed milk and peanut butter in the top of a double boiler over simmering water or in a very heavy 1-quart saucepan over very low heat. Cook, stirring constantly, until the mixture thickens, about 15 minutes in a double boiler or about 5 minutes over direct heat. Cool 10 minutes and use to fill and frost a 2-layer cake.

Frosts and fills an 8-inch 2-layer cake

"Standard measuring cups and spoons should be used when baking cakes. All ingredients are measured level."
—*Down-On-The-Farm Cook Book,* 1943

★ ★ ★ ★ ★ ★ Victory Frosting ★ ★ ★ ★ ★ ★

This "sugarless" recipe appeared in many guises during the war but the proportions were the same—one cup of whatever sweet syrup you could get and two egg whites.

1 cup light or dark corn syrup, or
    maple syrup, or melted jelly
2 egg whites

1 teaspoon vanilla
⅛ teaspoon salt

Bring syrup to a boil over low heat; simmer 3 minutes.

Combine egg whites, vanilla, and salt in the top of a double boiler; place over simmering water and beat with an electric mixer on high speed adding hot syrup in a steady stream. Continue beating until frosting is thick and reaches 160°F. Use to fill and frost a 2-layer cake.

Marble Topping: While the frosting is hot; grate 1 (1-ounce) square semi-sweet chocolate over the top of cake and allow to melt. Swirl chocolate into frosting to marbleize.

Makes enough for a 2-layer cake

 "Those exasperating cake failures often can be traced to inaccurate measurements."—*Good Housekeeping*, April 1943

★ ★ ★ ★ ★ ★ ★ ★ Fillings ★ ★ ★ ★ ★ ★ ★ ★ ★

If something other than frosting could be used to fill a 2-layer cake, it would reduce the strain on the "sugar book." Here are some of the options for home bakers on the home front:

Cranberry Filling: Combine 1 cup whole berry cranberry sauce and 4 teaspoons cornstarch in a small saucepan. Cook, stirring constantly, until the mixture is thickened. Cool before using to fill a holiday cake.

Berries-and-Cream Filling: Stir together ½ cup sweetened condensed milk and 2 tablespoons lemon juice in a small bowl until it thickens. Fold in ½ cup raspberries, blueberries, or sliced strawberries and it's ready to use.

Prune Filling: Combine ¾ cup water and ½ cup quartered, seeded prunes in a small saucepan; simmer until prunes are tender, about 5 minutes. Stir together 2 tablespoons light corn syrup, 1 tablespoon lemon juice, and 2 teaspoons cornstarch in a cup; stir into prune mixture and cook, stirring until mixture is thick.

Pineapple Filling: Combine an 8-ounce can crushed pineapple in heavy syrup, 1 tablespoon cornstarch, and ½ teaspoon ground ginger in a small saucepan. Cook over low heat, stirring constantly until thickened. Cool to room temperature before using.

Walnut Filling: Combine 1 cup finely chopped walnuts, ¼ cup water, and 2 tablespoons light or dark corn syrup in a small saucepan. Cook over low heat, stirring until mixture is thick. Remove from heat and stir in ¼ teaspoon imitation black walnut extract or ½ teaspoon vanilla extract.

Each makes ¾ to 1 cup

Melody Mélange

The caption for this dessert from the March 1943 Woman's Home Companion *suggested that "a rich finale picks up an otherwise plain-fare menu." The sponge cake layers were purchased and then dressed up with a filling that the recipe said could be made two to three days ahead. Although the recipe didn't recommend refrigeration, I would say it is mandatory!*

1½ cups milk

½ cup sugar

¼ cup unsifted all-purpose flour

¼ teaspoon salt

1 teaspoon vanilla extract

⅓ cup margarine or softened butter (or a mixture)

½ teaspoon almond extract

1 (1-ounce) square unsweetened chocolate, melted

2 round sponge or other cake layers, split crosswise

1 cup crushed almond or peanut brittle

Bring milk to a boil in a medium saucepan over very low heat or in the top of a double boiler over simmering water.

Combine sugar, flour, and salt in a small bowl. Gradually beat the hot milk into the sugar mixture and return to saucepan. Cook, stirring constantly, until a thickened pudding forms. Cover and cook 15 minutes longer, stirring occasionally. Add vanilla and cool to room temperature.

Beat margarine or butter in a medium bowl with an electric mixer. Gradually beat in cooled pudding with mixer on low speed. Remove ⅓ of mixture to a small bowl; stir in almond extract. Add melted chocolate to the remaining pudding.

Place the bottom of one cake layer on serving plate, spread with some of chocolate pudding. Add top of layer and frost with half of almond pudding; repeat with remaining layer.

Frost sides of cake with remaining chocolate pudding and refrigerate until ready to serve. Sprinkle with peanut brittle just before serving. Store any leftovers in the refrigerator.

10 to 12 Servings

3

★ ★ ★ ★ Precious Pastries ★ ★ ★ ★

PIES AND TARTS

Shortcut Pastry Mix	Patriot's Pie
Apple Dumpling Pie	Pumpkin Pie
Apricot-Peach Pie	"Sugarless" Custard Pie
Butterscotch Pie	"Sugarless" Fresh Berry Pie
Citrus Meringue Pie	Banana Dumplings
Cottage Cheese Pie	Berry-Cheese Tarts
Nut Pie	Tea Party Tarts

WARTIME SPECIAL
Raspberry-Applesauce Pie

CAN ALL YOU CAN

IT'S A REAL WAR JOB!

 "If every woman, every day, in everything she does, will do her utmost to accomplish the aims of our Government, then that combined effort will soon become a gigantic and valuable aid toward winning this war."—Victory Binding of the American Woman's Cook Book, 1942

PIE BAKING WAS LABELED an indulgence during the war because of the amount of shortening it takes to make a tender, flaky double-crust pie and because it was perceived as more time-consuming than making some other baked goods. Homemakers were told that it was patriotic to make single crust pies because they used half the shortening required for a double crust pie. And recipes for homemade pastry mixes appeared in women's magazines to cut down on the preparation time of making individual crusts. All of the pastry crusts in this chapter call for the Shortcut Pastry Mix that appears on page 52, and they have been tested in standard pie plates. While you can certainly substitute one of today's pastry shortcuts, be sure to use standard pie plates, as today's aluminum-foil ones hold less filling.

While many bakers were still comfortable using lard for their pastry, vegetable shortening had been around since before the First World War, was promoted as more dependable for pastry, and was the preferred fat, after butter, if there was a choice. Fats were rationed in February of 1943 with the introduction of Point Rationing and War Ration Book II. This was the first rationing program in which people could choose which of the covered items they wanted to "buy" with their coupons. Shortening and vegetable oils were generally available, reasonably priced, and required fewer ration points than other items in their category, so pie baking continued to the delight of American families. Cookie and graham cracker–crumb crusts became popular as well, because the sugar and shortening they contained came from the manufacturer's ration, not from the homemaker's.

The pies that follow show more wartime influence in the fillings than in the crusts. They feature simple, low-sugar puddings, custards, and dried fruit fillings made from staple ingredients that were likely to be in the pantry at all times. Fresh fruit and commercially canned fruit were scarce unless they were produced locally or home-canned. Pies, particularly double-crust pies, were most likely to be on the menu in magazine articles around holidays such as Thanksgiving, the February presidents' birthdays, and Easter.

★ ★ ★ ★ ★ ★ Shortcut Pastry Mix ★ ★ ★ ★ ★ ★

Busy wartime homemakers were still expected to bake several pies a week for their families. This make-ahead pastry mix from a vegetable shortening advertisement was very popular because it gave a head start for preparing the pastry. The advertisement featured a kindly aunt advising, "Now it's so easy to give your men folks all the pies they want."

7 cups unsifted all-purpose flour	1 tablespoon sugar
1 tablespoon salt	1 (1-pound) can vegetable shortening

Combine flour, salt, and sugar in a large bowl. Add half of the shortening; cut shortening into dry ingredients with pastry blender or two knives used scissors fashion until mixture is the consistency of cornmeal. Add remaining half of shortening and cut into dry ingredients until the size of green peas. Store in a tightly-closed container in a cool part of the kitchen.

To make the pastry for a double-crust pie or 8 tart shells, measure 3 cups of mix into a medium bowl and stir in about 5 tablespoons ice water using a fork. Press mixture together to make 2 flattened balls of pastry. Roll out and fill as directed in pie recipe. Use half recipe for a single-crust pie.

7 (10- to 11-inch) pastry rounds

"The first step in making good pie crust is to have the water and shortening very cold. The next thing to be remembered is to handle the dough as little as possible, chop the ingredients together, like mixing mortar, instead of kneading as in mixing bread doughs."
—*Army Mess Management Simplified*, 1942

★ ★ ★ ★ ★ ★ Apple Dumpling Pie ★ ★ ★ ★ ★ ★

This pastry technique, often called "country style" these days, is used to give a pie a rustic look. But in the October 1944 issue of Good Housekeeping, *it was recommended because it had the advantages of a double-crust pie yet required less pastry, therefore less shortening, and was faster to put together.*

⅓ cup packed light brown sugar

2 tablespoons all-purpose flour

½ teaspoon ground cinnamon

2 pounds (about 8 medium) cooking
   apples, peeled and sliced

2 cups Shortcut Pastry Mix
   (page 52)

3 to 4 tablespoons ice water

1 tablespoon butter, thinly sliced

Stir together brown sugar, flour, and cinnamon in a large bowl. Add apples and toss to combine.

Preheat oven to 425°F. Stir together pastry mix and ice water in a medium bowl; press together to make a flattened ball. Roll out pastry to a 14-inch round; trim edge neatly. Transfer to a 9-inch pie plate, allowing excess pastry to extend over edge of pie plate. Transfer apple mixture to pie plate; top with butter. Carefully lift overhanging pastry over the apple filling, overlapping where necessary and leaving an open space in the center.

Place pie on a rimmed baking sheet and bake until crust is golden and the filling bubbles through the center hole, about 40 minutes. Cool at least 30 minutes before cutting.

6 Servings

"IN PASTRY: Use lard or vegetable shortening. If these are not available, bacon fat, or poultry fat, or clarified drippings may be used."—*Your Share,* 1943

★ ★ ★ ★ ★ ★ Apricot-Peach Pie ★ ★ ★ ★ ★ ★

Dried apricots bring so much flavor to this pie that you almost think the fruit is fresh from the orchard. But because the pie uses dried fruit, which was plentiful during the war, and home-canned peaches, it was a home-front favorite that could be baked at any time of the year. In addition, making use of some of the heavy syrup from the canned peaches meant that the recipe could call for only ¼ cup of the rationed, granulated sugar.

1½ cups dried apricots, halved

½ cup water

1 quart peaches canned in heavy
  syrup

1 tablespoon grated lemon peel

3 tablespoons lemon juice

¼ teaspoon salt

¼ cup sugar

3 tablespoons unsifted all-purpose
  flour

Shortcut Pastry Mix for double-
  crust pie (page 52)

Bring apricots and water to a boil in a large saucepan over medium heat; cover and set aside 5 minutes. Drain peaches, reserving syrup. Stir peaches, ⅔ cup reserved syrup, the lemon peel and juice, and salt into the apricots. Stir together sugar and flour in a small bowl; stir into apricot-peach mixture until thoroughly blended. Cook, stirring constantly, just until the mixture begins to thicken, 3 to 5 minutes. Set aside to cool slightly, about 10 minutes.

Meanwhile, prepare pastry following recipe directions. Preheat oven to 375°F. Roll out half of pastry to an 11-inch round. Transfer to a 9-inch pie plate; fill with apricot-peach filling. Moisten edge of pastry.

Roll out remaining half of pastry to a 10-inch round. With a 2-inch cookie cutter, cut and remove a seasonal design from the center of the pastry round. Place crust over filling, centering cutout design. Turn excess pastry under and flute edge.

Bake pie until crust is golden and the filling bubbles through the center hole—40 to 45 minutes. Cool 15 minutes before cutting. Store any leftovers in the refrigerator.

6 Servings

★ ★ ★ ★ ★ ★ Butterscotch Pie ★ ★ ★ ★ ★ ★ ★

This butterscotch pie has only enough butter in it to keep the name, but it is certainly an easy-to-fix dessert, and the filling would be delicious in a bowl as well.

Shortcut Pastry Mix for single-crust
   pie (page 52)
1 cup packed light brown sugar
⅓ cup flour
½ teaspoon salt
1¾ cups milk or half-and-half

1 large egg
1 tablespoon butter
½ cup heavy cream
1 teaspoon granulated sugar
½ teaspoon vanilla extract

Preheat oven to 425°F. Prepare pastry following recipe directions. Roll out pastry to a 10-inch round. Transfer to an 8-inch pie plate; turn excess pastry under and flute edge. Pierce bottom and side with tines of a fork. Add pie weights, if desired and bake until golden, about 10 minutes. If using pie weights, remove for the last 2 to 3 minutes.

Meanwhile, combine brown sugar, flour, and salt in a medium saucepan; gradually stir in 1½ cups milk. Bring mixture to a boil over low heat, stirring constantly, until a thickened pudding forms. Beat egg and remaining ¼ cup milk in a small bowl; beat in about ½ cup of the pudding. Return mixture to saucepan and stir until thoroughly blended. Return just to a boil; remove from heat and stir in butter. Transfer to baked pastry shell and cool to room temperature. Refrigerate until ready to serve.

Just before serving, combine cream, granulated sugar, and vanilla in a small bowl and beat until stiff peaks form. Spoon around edge of pie to make a border. Cut into 6 wedges and serve. Store any leftovers in the refrigerator.

6 Servings

★ ★ ★ ★ ★ Citrus Meringue Pie ★ ★ ★ ★ ★

A combination of citrus juices gives this meringue pie a fresh, tangy flavor. It gets most of its sweetness from corn syrup, which is even used in the meringue.

Shortcut Pastry Mix for single-crust pie (page 52)
2 large eggs, separated
¼ cup water
⅓ cup cornstarch
¼ cup sugar
¾ cup orange juice
½ cup grapefruit juice
1¼ cups corn syrup
1 teaspoon grated lemon peel
¼ cup lemon juice
1 tablespoon butter

Preheat oven to 425°F. Prepare pastry following recipe directions. Roll out pastry to a 10-inch round. Transfer to an 8-inch pie plate; turn excess pastry under and flute edge. Pierce bottom and side with tines of a fork. Add pie weights, if desired, and bake until golden, about 10 minutes. If using pie weights, remove for the last 2 to 3 minutes. Reduce oven temperature to 350°F.

Meanwhile, combine egg yolks and water and set aside. Combine cornstarch and sugar in a heavy saucepan; gradually stir in orange and grapefruit juices until cornstarch is completely integrated. Stir in 1 cup corn syrup and bring to a boil over medium heat, stirring constantly. When mixture has thickened, stir in egg yolk mixture and cook, stirring constantly until mixture just begins to return to a boil. Do not allow to actually boil. Remove from heat and stir in lemon peel, lemon juice, and butter. Transfer to pastry crust.

Beat the egg whites in a small bowl with an electric mixer on high speed until soft peaks form. Gradually add the remaining ¼ cup corn syrup, beating until stiff meringue forms; spread meringue over pie. Bake 10 to 12 minutes or until well browned.

Cool to room temperature and refrigerate until ready to serve. Store any leftovers in the refrigerator.

6 Servings

★ ★ ★ ★ ★ ★ Cottage Cheese Pie ★ ★ ★ ★ ★ ★

Cheese pie was my favorite from our local bakery, and I could never quite recreate it until I found this recipe in a cookbook distributed by the dairy my father had worked for. We seemed to have a plentiful supply of cottage cheese at our house in those days; cottage cheese was not rationed because it was so perishable that it would have been difficult to ship overseas.

1½ cups graham cracker crumbs

¼ cup vegetable shortening or
    butter (or a mixture), melted

2 tablespoons packed light brown
    sugar

½ cup granulated sugar

3 tablespoons unsifted all-purpose
    flour

1 cup creamed cottage cheese

3 large eggs

¾ cup milk

1 teaspoon grated lemon peel

3 tablespoons lemon juice

1 teaspoon vanilla extract

Preheat oven to 350°F. Generously grease an 8-inch pie plate. Combine graham cracker crumbs, melted shortening, and brown sugar in a small bowl; transfer to greased pie plate and pat to line bottom and side of plate, making a rim on the edge.

Stir granulated sugar and flour together in a medium bowl until flour is thoroughly blended. Add cottage cheese and beat with an electric mixer at high speed until smooth. Gradually beat in eggs, then milk, lemon peel and juice, and vanilla.

Transfer cottage cheese mixture to graham cracker crust and bake until center of filling seems set, about 45 minutes.

Cool to room temperature before cutting. Store any leftovers in the refrigerator.

6 Servings

★ ★ ★ ★ ★ ★ ★ ★ ★ ★ Nut Pie ★ ★ ★ ★ ★ ★ ★ ★ ★ ★

Nuts were recommended as good sources of protein during the war. This wartime favorite is really a traditional brown sugar-pecan pie recipe accompanied by permission to use whatever nuts you can get. If pecans aren't in the market, don't fret, use walnuts, almonds, hazelnuts, pine nuts, peanuts, or a mixture.

Shortcut Pastry Mix for single-crust
   pie (page 52)
3/4 cup packed light brown sugar
1 tablespoon unsifted all-purpose
   flour
1 cup light corn syrup

3 large eggs
1 tablespoon butter, melted
1 teaspoon vanilla
1/4 teaspoon salt
1 cup pecans or other nuts or a
   mixture

Preheat oven to 350°F. Prepare pastry following recipe directions; roll out to an 11-inch round. Transfer to a 9-inch pie plate; turn excess pastry under and flute edge.

Stir brown sugar and flour together in a medium bowl until flour is thoroughly blended. Add corn syrup, eggs, butter, vanilla, and salt; beat with an electric mixer at high speed until smooth. Fold in nuts.

Place crust-lined pie plate on a rimmed baking sheet. Carefully transfer nut mixture to pastry crust. Bake pie until crust is golden and filling is set, about 50 minutes.

Cool to room temperature before cutting. Store any leftovers in the refrigerator.

6 Servings

"Salvaging Waste Fats is Vital to Victory: They are urgently needed to make the glycerin used in explosives and other munitions of war."—*Good Housekeeping*, July 1943

★ ★ ★ ★ ★ ★ ★ Patriot's Pie ★ ★ ★ ★ ★ ★ ★

This orange-flavored raisin pie appeared in a vegetable shortening advertisement for the February 1945 presidents' birthdays as an alternate for the usual cherry pie. Because most commercially canned foods were going to the armed forces and our allies in Europe, there would be few cherry pies in America, with the exception of those made by homemakers who had their own supply of home-canned cherries.

1½ cups dark seedless raisins	1 teaspoon grated orange peel
1½ cups water	1 teaspoon grated lemon peel
¼ cup orange juice	½ teaspoon salt
1 tablespoon lemon juice	Shortcut Pastry Mix for double-
⅓ cup packed light brown sugar	crust pie (page 52)
2 tablespoons all-purpose flour	2 maraschino cherries

Combine raisins, water, orange juice, and lemon juice in a medium saucepan. Bring to a boil over high heat; reduce heat to low and simmer until raisins are tender, about 5 minutes.

Stir together brown sugar, flour, orange and lemon peel, and salt in a small bowl until flour is thoroughly mixed into other ingredients. Stir brown-sugar mixture into raisin mixture and set aside to cool slightly, 15 to 20 minutes. Meanwhile, prepare pastry following recipe directions.

Preheat oven to 375°F. Roll out half of pastry to a 10-inch round. Transfer to an 8-inch pie plate; fill with raisin filling. Moisten edge of pastry. Roll out remaining half of pastry to a 10-inch round. Draw 2 cherry leaves and stems in center of crust with the tip of a knife. Cut out a ¾-inch round at the end of each cherry stem. Place crust over filling, centering cherry design. Turn excess pastry under and flute edge. Press a maraschino cherry into each hole in crust.

Bake pie until crust is golden and the filling bubbles around the cherries—about 45 minutes. Cool 30 minutes before cutting. Store any leftovers in the refrigerator.

6 Servings

★ ★ ★ ★ ★ ★ ★ Pumpkin Pie ★ ★ ★ ★ ★ ★ ★ ★

Autumn celebrations just wouldn't be the same without pumpkin pie, and a pumpkin from the Victory Garden or a supply of home-canned pumpkin puree meant that the traditional dessert could be on the table even if the turkey was made of Spam. My family has been using this recipe ever since I can remember. Because the egg whites are beaten separately, the filling bakes to form two layers, a fluffy layer on top and the usual custardlike layer at the bottom. One can of pumpkin puree will still work in the recipe, even though the volume per can now measures less than 2 cups.

Shortcut Pastry Mix for single-crust
    pie (page 52)
2 large eggs, separated
2 cups homemade or 1 can
    (15 ounces) pumpkin puree

1 cup packed light brown sugar
1 teaspoon ground cinnamon
1 teaspoon ground ginger
1/2 teaspoon salt
1 cup milk

Preheat oven to 375°F. Prepare pastry following recipe directions; roll out to an 11-inch round. Transfer to a 9-inch pie plate; turn excess pastry under and flute edge.

Beat egg whites in a medium bowl with an electric mixer until just stiff. With same beaters, beat pumpkin, egg yolks, brown sugar, cinnamon, ginger, and salt in a large bowl. Gradually beat in milk. Fold in beaten whites and transfer to pastry crust.

Bake pie until crust is golden and filling is set, about 45 minutes.

Cool 30 minutes before cutting. Store any leftovers in the refrigerator.

6 Servings

★ ★ ★ ★ ★ "Sugarless" Custard Pie ★ ★ ★ ★ ★

When it was available, sweetened condensed milk was an excellent way to sweeten desserts during wartime. Using it often simplified the recipe as well.

Shortcut Pastry Mix for single-crust
   pie (page 52)
2 cups boiling water
²/₃ cup sweetened condensed milk
3 large eggs

2 teaspoons vanilla extract
¼ teaspoon salt
⅛ teaspoon ground nutmeg,
   optional

Preheat oven to 400°F. Prepare pastry following recipe directions; roll out to an 11-inch round. Transfer to a 9-inch pie plate; turn excess pastry under and flute edge.

Combine water and sweetened condensed milk in a medium bowl. Beat eggs, vanilla, and salt in a large bowl with a whisk. Gradually beat in milk mixture until thoroughly blended. Transfer to pastry crust; sprinkle with nutmeg, if desired.

Bake pie 5 minutes. Reduce oven temperature to 325°F and bake until crust is golden and filling is set, 35 to 40 minutes longer.

Cool to room temperature before cutting. Store any leftovers in the refrigerator.

6 Servings

"No set number of points are designated for fats and cheese. It is left to every homemaker to distribute her points wisely between meat, fat and cheese."—*69 Ration Recipes for Meat*, 1942

★ ★ ★ "Sugarless" Fresh Berry Pie ★ ★ ★

When berries were in season they were often free for the picking, and a fresh berry pie was a very special treat indeed. Sweetening it with corn syrup, rather than granulated sugar, made it easier on the pocketbook and ration book.

Shortcut Pastry mix for double-
   crust pie (page 52)

1¼ cups light corn syrup

½ cup unsifted all-purpose flour

1 tablespoon lemon juice

⅛ teaspoon salt

4 cups berries, rinsed and drained

Preheat oven to 375°F. Prepare pastry following recipe directions. Combine corn syrup, flour, lemon juice, and salt in a large bowl; fold in berries.

Roll out half of pastry to an 11-inch round. Transfer to a 9-inch pie plate; fill with berry mixture. Moisten edge of pastry. Roll out remaining half of pastry to a 10-inch round; cut out a ¾-inch hole in the center. Place crust over filling, centering hole. Turn excess pastry under and flute edge.

Bake pie until crust is golden and the filling bubbles in the center hole—about 45 minutes.

Cool 30 minutes before cutting. Store any leftovers in the refrigerator.

6 Servings

"Not many know how to make a good flaky pie crust, and very few make a pie day after day, which has the same fine uniformity. This is due to careless-ness in measuring the ingredients necessary to make these pies."—*Hamilton Ross Modern Cook Book,* 1940

★ ★ ★ ★ ★ ★ Banana Dumplings ★ ★ ★ ★ ★ ★ ★

In wartime households everyone was encouraged to pitch in. Many food articles offered recipes that could be made by children as young as six. This recipe is so easy, even younger children would love to help with assembly, as long as someone older takes care of the baking.

Shortcut Pastry Mix for single-crust pie (page 52)

2 tablespoons packed light brown sugar

$\frac{1}{2}$ teaspoon ground cinnamon

4 ripe bananas, peeled

Heavy cream, optional (see Note)

Preheat oven to 375°F. Grease a small, rimmed baking sheet. Prepare pastry following recipe directions.

Roll out pastry to a 14- by 6-inch rectangle. Sprinkle with brown sugar and cinnamon; pat sugar mixture onto pastry and cut lengthwise into four 1½-inch-wide strips. Spiral-wrap one strip around each banana, sugar side in, to cover completely and place on baking sheet with end of strip down.

Bake until pastry is golden, 20 to 25 minutes; serve warm with cream, if desired. Store any leftovers in the refrigerator.

NOTE: We found them delicious with fudge or fresh raspberry sauce, which would have been hard to come by at the time.

4 Servings

 "Cakes and Pies and Real Home Fries . . . that's what a G.I. dreams of! Lady—make his dreams come true!"—Crisco advertisement, January 1946

★ ★ ★ ★ ★ ★ Berry-Cheese Tarts ★ ★ ★ ★ ★ ★ ★

This recipe, based on one in the May 1943 issue of Good Housekeeping, *was unusual in that it called for "quick-frozen" berries, truly a gourmet product at the time, and fresh ones as a second choice. Although the results are best if assembled shortly before serving, the shells can be made a day ahead and stored at room temperature, and the filling and berries can be prepared several hours ahead and refrigerated.*

Shortcut Pastry Mix for double-
   crust pie (page 52)
1 (8-ounce) package cream cheese,
   softened
2 tablespoons honey

1 tablespoon half-and-half
2 cups thawed frozen or 1 pint fresh
   berries
2 tablespoons currant jelly, melted

Preheat oven to 425°F. Prepare pastry following recipe directions. Divide into 8 balls; roll out each to make a 6-inch round. Fit pastry rounds into eight 3-inch fluted tart shells; pierce bottoms and sides with tines of a fork. Place on baking sheets for easy handling and bake until golden, 8 to 10 minutes.

Remove tart shells in pans to cooling racks and cool to room temperature. When shells are cool, remove to serving tray.

No more than 30 minutes before serving, stir together cream cheese, honey, and half-and-half. Drain frozen berries or rinse and drain fresh ones. (If using large strawberries, halve or quarter.)

Divide cream cheese mixture among shells; top with berries, brush with jelly, and serve. Store any leftovers in the refrigerator.

8 Servings

★ ★ ★ ★ ★ ★ ★ Tea Party Tarts ★ ★ ★ ★ ★ ★ ★

These biscuit tarts are so easy to make that this is a good recipe for young bakers to prepare for an afternoon tea party. The tarts were featured in a corn syrup advertisement as the morale-lifting dessert after a very spare wartime meatless meal.

1 cup finely chopped pecans or walnuts

½ cup dark corn syrup

2 tablespoons heavy cream or undiluted evaporated milk

½ teaspoon vanilla extract

¼ teaspoon cinnamon

2 cups unsifted all-purpose flour

2 tablespoons granulated sugar

4 teaspoons baking powder

½ teaspoon salt

⅓ cup vegetable shortening or butter (or a mixture)

¾ cup milk

18 pecan or walnut halves

Preheat oven to 425°F. Lightly grease 2 baking sheets. Combine nuts, corn syrup, cream, vanilla, and cinnamon for filling; set aside. Combine flour, sugar, baking powder, and salt in a medium bowl; cut in shortening with a pastry blender or two knives until coarse crumbs forms. Stir in the milk just until biscuit dough forms.

Turn dough out onto a floured board and knead into a ball. Roll dough out ⅛ inch thick. Cut out as many 3-inch rounds as possible. Cut out and remove a 2-inch round from the center of 18 rounds to make rings. Reroll removed dough and cut rounds until you have 18 solid rounds. Place the solid rounds on greased baking sheets; spread with half of the nut filling. Top each with a biscuit ring. Spoon remaining nut mixture into centers of rings and top each with a nut.

Bake for 12 to 15 minutes or until lightly browned.

Cool 15 minutes on baking sheet; serve warm or at room temperature.

18 Servings

Raspberry-Applesauce Pie

A gelatin mix supplies sweetness and flavor for this easy pie. This wartime technique for sweetening without the use of ration coupons was used for cakes, candy, and fruit punch as well. The original recipe suggested serving it as a Valentine's Day dessert.

Shortcut Pastry Mix for single-crust
   pie (page 52)
3½ cups sweetened applesauce
1 (3-ounce) package raspberry-
   flavored gelatin mix

1 envelope unflavored gelatin
Cream Cheese Topping, recipe
   follows

Preheat oven to 425°F. Prepare pastry following recipe directions. Roll out pastry to an 11-inch round. Transfer to a 9-inch pie plate; turn excess pastry under and flute edge. Pierce bottom and side with tines of a fork. Add pie weights, if desired, and bake until golden, about 10 minutes. If using pie weights, remove for the last 2 to 3 minutes.

Bring applesauce to a boil in a medium saucepan over low heat, stirring constantly; remove from heat. Combine gelatin mix and unflavored gelatin; stir into applesauce until gelatin has dissolved. Transfer mixture to crust; refrigerate until firm, about 2 hours.

Cut into 6 wedges and add cream cheese topping. Store any leftovers in the refrigerator.

Cream Cheese Topping: Stir together 1 (3-ounce) package cream cheese, softened, 1 tablespoon honey, and 2 to 3 teaspoons heavy cream until mixture is consistency of heavy cream. Refrigerate until ready to serve.

6 Servings

4

★ ★ ★ ★ By Hand or by Sea ★ ★ ★ ★

COOKIES FOR HOME OR ABROAD

Apple Butter Cookies	*Gingersnaps*
Brazil Nut Snaps	*Oatmeal Icebox Cookies*
Butterscotch Squares	*Peanut Brownies*
Carrot Cookies	*Peanut Butter Cookies*
Chocolate Rolled Oats Cookies	*Prune Drops*
Chocolate Sticks	*Spiced Wafers*
Crybabies	*Sugar Cookies*
Date Bars	*Walnutaroons*
Dried Fruit Bars	*War Shortbread*

WARTIME SPECIAL

Coconut or Nut Fingers

EVERY CHILD NEEDS A GOOD SCHOOL LUNCH

THE WAR FOOD ADMINISTRATION WILL HELP YOUR COMMUNITY START A

SCHOOL LUNCH PROGRAM

"You can stuff yourself with food . . . eat so much you can hardly walk away from the table . . . and still be <u>committing dietary suicide!</u> Surveys show that millions of Americans are not getting all the vitamins they need." —Canned Florida Citrus Fruits advertisement, July 1942

COOKIES WERE A STAPLE DESSERT in the early 1940s home. No matter how busy the family baker was, she was expected to have the cookie jar full at all times. However, cookie baking was affected by both sugar and butter rationing, as well as by a dwindling supply of spices. Happily, molasses, corn syrup, honey, and brown sugar saved the day and the addition of large quantities of dried fruit made the doughs go farther. The resulting cookies, although low in refined sugar and fat, were everything a wartime snack should be—nutritious, easily stored, and sturdy enough to be shipped overseas.

While most recipes called for vegetable shortening as a substitute for all or part of the butter they originally included, some cookie recipes specified margarine. This butter substitute was already being promoted as a nutritious food and recipes often called for "vitaminized" or "fortified" margarine. When talking to groups about the wartime kitchen, I find that one of the most vividly remembered wartime food experiences is of coloring the margarine. Butter manufacturers had convinced lawmakers to make it illegal to sell colored margarine, so it had to be colored at home. Eventually manufacturers included the food coloring in a separate section of the plastic packaging, and children fought over the privilege of popping the food coloring bubble and kneading the color into the margarine, which was still sealed in the sturdy plastic bag in which it was purchased.

Wartime cookie baking was also affected by the number of other responsibilities that suddenly competed for the home baker's time. Homemakers who might have previously turned out beautiful cutout and shaped cookies now opted to make bar cookies, drop cookies, and ice box cookies, which were more convenient. When magazine articles and advertisements did include a cutout cookie it was clearly intended for a special occasion, and the psychological benefit of sharing something special, something pretty, something from the good times before the war was stressed. The same respect was paid to Toll House cookies, which, at just over 10 years old, were still considered new. Because of the amount of butter, sugar, and chocolate they required, they were promoted as a very special gift for a serviceman, and occasionally to be given to children.

"Sugar was the rationed item that Americans told each other they missed most. Gallup invited respondents to fantasize near the war's end, asking which of four rationed commodities they would prefer. . . . 47% (almost half) opted for sugar."—From The Gallup Poll, quoted in *American Women and World War II*, 1990

★ ★ ★ ★ ★ Apple Butter Cookies ★ ★ ★ ★ ★

Sweet and spicy home-canned or commercially prepared apple butter makes an instant filling for these old-world filled cookies.

2 ½ cups unsifted all-purpose flour

½ teaspoon baking soda

½ teaspoon salt

¾ cup packed light brown sugar

½ cup vegetable shortening or
softened butter (or a mixture)

1 large egg

1 teaspoon vanilla extract

¼ cup buttermilk

½ cup apple butter

1 tablespoon granulated sugar,
optional

Grease two large baking sheets. Combine flour, soda, and salt in a small bowl.

Beat brown sugar and shortening in a medium bowl with an electric mixer until fluffy; beat in egg and vanilla. Add dry ingredients and buttermilk all at once; beat on low speed just until thoroughly blended. Form dough into a flattened ball. Roll out dough to ⅛-inch thickness between pieces of floured wax paper and cut out with 2½-inch round cutter; reroll to make a total of 48 rounds.

Preheat oven to 350°F. Divide apple butter onto the centers of 24 rounds. Moisten edge around apple butter and top each with another dough round. Press edge of each cookie with the tines of a fork to seal; place on greased baking sheets. Sprinkle tops with granulated sugar, if desired.

Bake cookies until golden brown at the edges, 12 to 15 minutes.

Cool completely on wire racks; serve or pack in an airtight container.

24 Cookies

★ ★ ★ ★ ★ ★ Brazil Nut Snaps ★ ★ ★ ★ ★ ★

The essential thing to remember when making these fragile cookies is to remove them from the baking sheet before they have a chance to stick. If the cookies do get cool, set them back in the oven for a minute to soften slightly. This recipe specifically called for margarine rather than vegetable shortening as a substitute for butter.

1¼ cups packed light brown sugar

¼ cup margarine or butter (or a mixture), melted

1 large egg

⅔ cup unsifted all-purpose flour

1 teaspoon baking powder

¼ teaspoon salt

1 cup chopped Brazil nuts, other nuts, or a mixture

Preheat oven to 325°F. Grease 2 baking sheets.

Combine brown sugar and margarine or butter in a medium bowl; beat with an electric mixer on high speed. Beat in egg. Add flour, baking powder, and salt and beat on low speed just until thoroughly blended. Fold in nuts.

Drop batter by teaspoonfuls onto greased baking sheets and bake until the edges begin to brown, 12 to 15 minutes.

Remove from baking sheet immediately and cool completely on a wire rack. Serve or pack in an airtight container.

36 Cookies

★ ★ ★ ★ ★ Butterscotch Squares ★ ★ ★ ★ ★

The brown sugar lends a mellow butterscotch flavor to these Blondies, even when they are made with vegetable shortening—although it is certainly more pronounced when made with the real thing. If tightly wrapped and still in their baking pan these ship well.

⅔ cup unsifted all-purpose flour	1 cup packed light brown sugar
½ teaspoon baking powder	2 large eggs
¼ teaspoon salt	⅓ cup evaporated milk
⅓ cup vegetable shortening or softened butter (or a mixture)	2 teaspoons vanilla extract
	1¼ cups chopped walnuts

Preheat oven to 350°F. Grease a 9-inch square baking pan. Sift or stir together the flour, baking powder, and salt.

Beat the shortening with an electric mixer on high speed until fluffy; gradually beat in the brown sugar. Add the eggs one at a time, beating well after each addition. Add the dry ingredients, milk, and vanilla; beat on low speed just until blended. Fold in walnuts.

Spoon the batter into the greased pan and bake 25 to 30 minutes or until the center appears set. Cut into 16 squares while warm. Cool completely and serve or store in an airtight container.

16 Servings

"Don't be a dog in the manger and buy rationed foods just for the sake of 'spending your points.' Destroy the stamps you don't need! Someone who really needs the items you don't buy will then find them on the grocer's shelf."—*Ladies' Home Journal*, October 1943

★ ★ ★ ★ ★ ★ ★ Carrot Cookies ★ ★ ★ ★ ★ ★ ★ ★

Carrots add sweetness and moisture to these spicy honey-sweetened drop cookies. The original recipe was described as "a neat camouflage for carrots."

<table>
<tr><td>3/4 cup honey</td><td>1 teaspoon ground cinnamon</td></tr>
<tr><td>2 large eggs</td><td>1/2 teaspoon salt</td></tr>
<tr><td>1/3 cup margarine or butter (or a mixture), softened</td><td>1/4 teaspoon baking soda</td></tr>
<tr><td></td><td>1/4 teaspoon ground nutmeg</td></tr>
<tr><td>1/4 cup milk</td><td>1 cup shredded carrots</td></tr>
<tr><td>2 cups unsifted all-purpose flour</td><td>1/3 cup dark seedless raisins</td></tr>
<tr><td>3 teaspoons baking powder</td><td>1/3 cup chopped nuts</td></tr>
</table>

Preheat oven to 375°F. Grease 2 baking sheets.

Beat honey and eggs until combined. Gradually beat in margarine or butter and milk. Stir flour, baking powder, cinnamon, salt, soda, and nutmeg into honey mixture until thoroughly blended. Fold in carrots, raisins, and nuts.

Drop batter by rounded teaspoonfuls onto greased baking sheets and bake 10 to 12 minutes or until a toothpick inserted in the center of one comes out clean. Remove to wire racks to cool. Repeat until all batter has been baked.

Cool completely and serve or pack in an airtight container and store in the refrigerator.

48 (3-inch) Cookies

★ ★ ★ Chocolate Rolled Oats Cookies ★ ★ ★

These honey-sweetened drop cookies are perfect for packing and shipping, as well as for filling home-front cookie jars with a nutritious snack.

2 cups unsifted all-purpose flour

½ teaspoon baking powder

½ teaspoon salt

¼ teaspoon baking soda

1 cup honey

⅓ cup vegetable shortening or butter (or a mixture), melted

2 (1-ounce) squares semisweet chocolate, melted

½ cup sour cream

1 large egg

2 teaspoons vanilla extract

1 cup quick-cooking rolled oats

½ cup dark seedless raisins

Preheat oven to 350°F. Grease 2 baking sheets. Stir together flour, baking powder, salt, and soda.

Beat together honey, shortening, and chocolate until combined; then beat in sour cream, egg, and vanilla. Stir in dry ingredients, oats, and raisins just until combined.

Drop dough by rounded teaspoonfuls onto greased baking sheets and bake 10 to 12 minutes or until lightly browned.

Cool on wire racks and serve or pack in an airtight container.

48 Cookies

"Because so much chocolate is going to our armed Forces as Emergency Rations, and the Nation's supply of cocoa beans is limited, we suggest reserving the restricted home supplies for the growing children."—Nestle's Cocoa advertisement, December 1943

★ ★ ★ ★ ★ ★ Chocolate Sticks ★ ★ ★ ★ ★ ★ ★

These holiday cookies are described as "canny users of your precious supplies of sugar and shortening" and the magazine article they appeared in gave packing directions so that they could be "sent to friends living at a distance."

1 cup unsifted all-purpose flour

1 teaspoon baking powder

½ teaspoon salt

¾ cup packed light brown sugar

¼ cup vegetable shortening or
softened butter (or a mixture)

1 large egg

1 teaspoon vanilla extract

1 (6-ounce) package semisweet
chocolate chips

¼ cup unsifted confectioners' sugar

Preheat oven to 350°F. Grease an 8-inch square baking pan. Combine flour, baking powder, and salt in a small bowl.

Beat brown sugar and shortening in a medium bowl with an electric mixer until fluffy; beat in egg and vanilla. Beat in dry ingredients until no flour is visible. Fold in chocolate chips and spoon into greased pan, then level the top surface with a spatula.

Bake 30 minutes or until golden brown.

Cool completely in pan; cut into 32 sticks, dust with confectioners' sugar and serve or pack in an airtight container.

32 Sticks

★ ★ ★ ★ ★ ★ ★ ★ Crybabies ★ ★ ★ ★ ★ ★ ★ ★ ★

I found these soft, spicy, molasses cookies in several wartime magazines with no explanation of their unusual name (in one article they were called Delaware Crybabies.) Something delicious you can bake when the cupboard is almost bare, these cookies are especially good for shipping.

2 cups unsifted all-purpose flour
1 teaspoon baking soda
1 teaspoon ground cinnamon
½ teaspoon ground nutmeg
¼ teaspoon salt
½ cup packed light brown sugar

½ cup vegetable shortening or
    softened butter (or a mixture),
    melted
½ cup light molasses
1 large egg
½ cup water

Preheat oven to 375°F. Grease 2 baking sheets. Stir together flour, soda, cinnamon, nutmeg, and salt.

Beat together brown sugar and shortening; beat in molasses and egg. Stir in dry ingredients alternately with water just until combined.

Drop batter by rounded teaspoonfuls onto greased baking sheets and bake 10 to 12 minutes or until a toothpick inserted in the center of one comes out clean.

Cool and serve or pack in an airtight container.

48 Cookies

★ ★ ★ ★ ★ ★ ★ ★ **Date Bars** ★ ★ ★ ★ ★ ★ ★ ★

There is no shortening or butter used in these easy-to-make bars. The original 1940s recipe recommends cutting the dates with a floured scissors, a trick that hasn't lost its effectiveness over the years.

⅓ cup unsifted all-purpose flour

1½ teaspoons baking powder

½ teaspoon ground cinnamon

¼ teaspoon ground nutmeg

¼ teaspoon salt

1 pound pitted dates, coarsely
   chopped

¾ cup chopped nuts

3 large eggs

⅓ cup packed light brown sugar

1 teaspoon vanilla extract

Preheat oven to 350°F. Grease a 9-inch square baking pan.

Combine flour, baking powder, cinnamon, nutmeg, and salt in a medium bowl. Add dates and nuts; stir together until dates are completely covered with dry ingredients.

Beat eggs in a medium bowl with an electric mixer; gradually beat in brown sugar and vanilla. Fold in date mixture until no flour is visible. Spoon date mixture into greased pan and level the top surface with a spatula.

Bake 20 to 25 minutes or until the center springs back when gently pressed.

Cool, cut into 20 bars and serve or store in an airtight container in the refrigerator.

20 Bars

 "U.S. housewives, who do the nation's buying, spend for food each year $14,753,000,000."—*Ladies' Home Journal,* August 1941

★ ★ ★ ★ ★ ★ Dried Fruit Bars ★ ★ ★ ★ ★ ★

Dried fruit seemed to always be available during the war and was a sweet addition to lots of cookie and cake recipes, including this one for moist bars that travel well.

1⅓ cups unsifted all-purpose flour

1 teaspoon ground ginger

½ teaspoon baking soda

¼ teaspoon salt

¼ cup packed light brown sugar

¼ cup light molasses

1 large egg

½ cup sour cream

1 cup coarsely chopped mixed dried
   fruit

½ cup chopped nuts

¾ cup unsifted confectioners' sugar

2 teaspoons water

1 teaspoon vanilla extract

Preheat oven to 400°F. Grease a 13- by 9-inch baking pan. Stir together the flour, ginger, soda, and salt.

Beat the brown sugar, molasses, and egg with an electric mixer on high speed until fluffy. Add the dry ingredients and sour cream; beat on low speed just until combined. Fold in dried fruit and nuts.

Transfer the batter to the greased pan and bake 12 to 15 minutes or until the center springs back when lightly pressed. Cool in pan 5 minutes. Combine confectioners' sugar, water, and vanilla in a small bowl to make a thick glaze. Spread over warm bars.

Cool to room temperature, cut and serve.

48 Bars

"It may not be convenient
But we don't admit defeat
For in spite of War and Rationing
America must eat!"—*Coupon Cookery*, 1943

★ ★ ★ ★ ★ ★ ★ Gingersnaps ★ ★ ★ ★ ★ ★ ★ ★

Wartime bakers found that gingersnaps could be made with a minimum of sugar, shortening, and effort, and they traveled well. These can be hand-shaped as directed, or rolled out and cut with cookie cutters when more time is available.

2 cups unsifted all-purpose flour

1 tablespoon ground ginger

1 teaspoon baking soda

1 teaspoon ground cinnamon

1/4 teaspoon salt

2/3 cup sugar

1/2 cup dark molasses

1/3 cup vegetable shortening or
   butter (or a mixture), melted

1 large egg, well beaten

Water for moistening hands

Preheat oven to 350°F. Grease 2 baking sheets. Stir together flour, ginger, soda, cinnamon, and salt in a small bowl.

Beat together sugar, molasses, shortening, and egg in a large bowl; stir in dry ingredients until thoroughly blended. Divide mixture into 48 mounds on a sheet of waxed paper.

With well-moistened hands, roll dough mounds into balls and place 2 inches apart on baking sheets.

Bake 10 to 12 minutes or until firm and crinkled.

Remove to wire racks to cool and repeat with remaining dough. Serve or pack in an airtight container.

48 Cookies

★ ★ ★ ★ ★ Oatmeal Icebox Cookies ★ ★ ★ ★ ★

While having a roll of cookie dough in the icebox was a big convenience to wartime homemakers, it is even more convenient these days, when the dough can be made ahead and kept in the freezer for up to three months instead of up to three days in a 1940s icebox.

2 cups quick-cooking rolled oats

1 cup unsifted all-purpose flour

3/4 cup packed light brown sugar

3/4 teaspoon baking soda

1/4 teaspoon salt

3/4 cup vegetable shortening or
  butter (or a mixture), melted

1/3 cup boiling water

Stir together the oats, flour, brown sugar, soda, and salt in a large bowl. Combine the shortening and water; gradually beat mixture into the oats mixture to form a stiff dough. Shape into a roll and wrap in waxed paper and then in plastic wrap. Refrigerate several hours or up to 3 days. May be kept in the freezer up to 3 months.

Preheat oven to 375°F. Grease 2 large baking sheets. Slice the oatmeal dough very thin and place 1 inch apart on baking sheets. Bake 8 to 10 minutes or until they begin to brown at the edges.

Remove to cooling rack and cool completely. Store in an airtight container.

48 cookies

"Cookies will keep well if stored in a tin box or a cooky [sic] jar.... Trying to save cookies is another matter. The only suggestion for that is a double lock on the pantry door!"
—*Down-On-The-Farm Cook Book*, 1943

★ ★ ★ ★ ★ ★ Peanut Brownies ★ ★ ★ ★ ★ ★

Wartime nutrition programs promoted peanuts as a good source of protein and B vitamins. Peanuts were added to everything from soups and stews to quick breads and pie crusts. These fudgy peanut brownies are a particularly delicious way to take your vitamins.

½ cup vegetable shortening or
   softened butter (or a mixture)

¾ cup sugar

3 (1-ounce) squares unsweetened
   chocolate, melted

2 large eggs

¼ cup unsifted all-purpose flour

2 teaspoons vanilla extract

⅛ teaspoon salt

1 cup chopped unsalted roasted
   peanuts

Preheat oven to 350°F. Grease a 9-inch square baking pan.

Beat the shortening in a medium bowl with an electric mixer on high speed until fluffy; gradually beat in the sugar and chocolate. Add the eggs one at a time, beating well after each addition. Add the flour, vanilla, and salt; beat on low speed just until blended. Fold in the peanuts.

Spread the dough into the greased pan and bake 25 to 30 minutes or until the center appears set. Cut into 16 squares while warm.

Cool completely and serve or store in an airtight container.

16 Servings

"Many of the old-time things have vanished from our everyday life, but the cookie jar has not been supplanted by something different—it occupies a more prominent place than ever."— *The Book of Cookies*, 1940

★ ★ ★ ★ ★ Peanut Butter Cookies ★ ★ ★ ★ ★

This recipe for the all-American favorite, peanut butter cookies, was ideal for wartime baking since it called for no butter or white granulated sugar and shipped remarkably well.

2 cups unsifted all-purpose flour	⅓ cup vegetable shortening or
1 teaspoon baking powder	butter (or a mixture), melted
½ teaspoon salt	½ cup packed light brown sugar
¼ teaspoon baking soda	¾ cup dark corn syrup
½ cup peanut butter	1 large egg

Preheat oven to 375°F. Grease 2 baking sheets. Stir together flour, baking powder, salt, and soda.

Beat together peanut butter, shortening, and brown sugar; beat in corn syrup and egg. Stir in dry ingredients just until combined.

Drop dough by rounded teaspoonfuls onto greased baking sheets; press with floured tines of fork in crisscross pattern and bake 10 to 12 minutes or until lightly browned.

Cool on wire racks and serve or pack in an airtight container.

48 Cookies

"In the war effort, fats are vital as (a) source of glycerine for explosives, drugs, and medical supplies. It is estimated that just one pound of waste fat makes enough glycerine to fire four 37 mm. anti-aircraft shells." —*69 Ration Recipes for Meat,* 1942

★ ★ ★ ★ ★ ★ ★ Prune Drops ★ ★ ★ ★ ★ ★ ★

Sweetened with honey and the concentrated fruit sugar of dried fruit, these high-fiber cookies were, and still are, the perfect healthy snack to pack for a busy day.

2/3 cup honey

2 large eggs

2/3 cup vegetable shortening or
   butter (or a mixture), melted

1/4 cup prune juice

2 cups unsifted all-purpose flour

4 teaspoons baking powder

1/2 teaspoon salt

1/4 teaspoon ground cloves

1 cup bran flakes cereal

1 cup moist pitted prunes, quartered

1/2 cup chopped dates

1/2 cup chopped nuts

Preheat oven to 375°F. Grease 2 baking sheets.

Beat honey and eggs until combined. Gradually beat in shortening and prune juice. Stir together flour, baking powder, salt, and cloves. Stir into honey mixture. Fold in cereal, prunes, dates, and nuts.

Drop dough by rounded teaspoonfuls onto greased baking sheets and bake 10 to 12 minutes or until a toothpick inserted in the center of one comes out clean.

Remove to cooling rack; repeat until all dough has been baked. Cool completely and serve or pack in an airtight container.

84 Cookies

★ ★ ★ ★ ★ ★ ★ Spiced Wafers ★ ★ ★ ★ ★ ★ ★

Ice-box cookies were a big help to homemakers balancing a factory or office job and a family at home that needed to be nurtured and fed according to government standards. These nutritious cookies can be prepared in the middle of the night and are ready to slice and bake whenever the family is able to get together for dinner.

2 cups unsifted all-purpose flour

2 teaspoons ground cinnamon

2 teaspoons ground ginger

1 teaspoon baking soda

1/4 teaspoon salt

1/2 cup packed light brown sugar

1/2 cup dark molasses

1/3 cup vegetable shortening or
   butter (or a mixture), melted

1 teaspoon vanilla extract

Stir together flour, cinnamon, ginger, baking soda, and salt.

Beat together brown sugar, molasses, shortening, and vanilla. Stir in dry ingredients just until combined. Divide mixture in half. Shape into two rolls and wrap in waxed paper and then in plastic wrap. Refrigerate several hours or up to 3 days. May be kept in the freezer up to 3 months.

To bake, preheat oven to 375°F. Grease 2 baking sheets. Thinly slice dough and arrange 1/2 inch apart on greased baking sheets. Bake 7 to 9 minutes or until lightly browned.

Cool on wire racks and serve or pack in an airtight container.

48 Cookies

★ ★ ★ ★ ★ ★ ★ Sugar Cookies ★ ★ ★ ★ ★ ★ ★

The December 1943 issue of Woman's Home Companion *ran a cookie article with a recipe that was low in sugar, a recipe that was low in shortening, a recipe for cookies that were "sturdy travelers," and these sugar cookies that are labeled "Easy to Look At." Although they don't meet the special criteria for wartime baked goods, these pretty little Christmas trees, Santas, and stars must have served to boost home-front morale over the holidays. In the 1940s the frosting would have been quite safely made with an egg white, but today we have opted for meringue powder that has been sterilized.*

1³/₄ cups unsifted all-purpose flour

1 teaspoon baking powder

¹/₄ teaspoon salt

³/₄ cup sugar

¹/₃ cup vegetable shortening or
    softened butter (or a mixture)

1 large egg

¹/₂ teaspoon almond extract

Frosting, optional, recipe follows

Colored sugar and decors, optional

Preheat oven to 400°F. Grease 2 baking sheets. Combine flour, baking powder, and salt in a small bowl.

Beat sugar and shortening in a medium bowl with an electric mixer until fluffy; beat in egg and almond extract. Beat in dry ingredients until no flour is visible. Roll out to ¹/₈-inch thickness between pieces of floured waxed paper and cut out with 2-inch holiday cutters.

Bake 6 to 8 minutes or until golden brown at the edges.

Cool completely on wire racks; frost and decorate if desired. Serve, or pack in an airtight container.

Frosting: Combine 1 cup unsifted confectioners' sugar, 2 tablespoons water, and 1 tablespoon meringue powder in a medium bowl. Beat with an electric mixer until stiff points form. Divide into small dishes; stir in **food coloring** and just enough drops of water to make the frosting flow. Spread or brush over cookies. If you are using more than one color on a cookie, let the first dry completely before adding the second.

48 Small Cookies

 "In the point rationing system the government allows a specified number of points per person per period, 48 points have been allotted for the first period. Thus, if you have 5 persons in your family it means you have a total of 240 points to spend."—"Points About Points," *Woman's Home Companion*, April 1943

★ ★ ★ ★ ★ ★ Walnutaroons ★ ★ ★ ★ ★ ★ ★

This five-ingredient recipe couldn't be easier. The resulting walnut macaroons are an elegant golden color from the brown sugar.

1 large egg white

3/4 cup packed light brown sugar

1 cup chopped walnuts or other nuts

1/2 teaspoon vanilla extract

1/8 teaspoon salt

Preheat oven to 350°F. Line 2 baking sheets with parchment or aluminum foil; grease generously.

Beat egg white until stiff but not dry; gradually fold in the brown sugar, walnuts, vanilla, and salt.

Drop batter by teaspoonfuls onto prepared baking sheets to make 24 mounds. Bake until light brown, 15 to 20 minutes. Cool on pans 3 or 4 minutes.

Remove to wire racks and cool completely; serve or pack in an airtight container.

24 Cookies

 In the early 1940s, *Woman's Home Companion* readers were fascinated by Aunt Em, whose recipes and baking advice appeared frequently in the magazine. Apparently, some skeptical readers had written to Nell B. Nichols, Field Editor of the Home Service Center, accusing her of making up the character. The editors responded with a special "Salute to Aunt Em," telling readers that "Aunt Em was as real and substantial as the food for which she was famous" and that she had been Mrs. Nichols's inspiration as a cook.

★ ★ ★ ★ ★ ★ War Shortbread ★ ★ ★ ★ ★ ★

Despite the flavor supplied by the brown sugar, these delicate cookies do have less flavor when made entirely with shortening. A quick wartime trick that helps is to spread the top of the cookies with just a little butter as they come out of the oven. This can even be done by rubbing them gently with the waxed paper wrapper from a stick of butter.

½ cup vegetable shortening or softened butter (or a mixture)

½ cup packed light brown sugar

2½ cups old-fashioned rolled oats, ground or chopped in a processor

Preheat oven to 350°F. Grease two 9-inch round baking pans; line bottoms with aluminum foil or parchment and grease foil.

Stir together shortening and brown sugar in a medium bowl with a fork until smooth. Stir in oats until thoroughly blended.

Divide dough in half and pat out half in each prepared pan to make a level surface. Bake 15 to 20 minutes or until beginning to brown and firm to the touch. Cut each pan into 8 wedges while warm.

Cool completely and serve or store in an airtight container.

16 Cookies

 "Military Christmas Cookies: It will be a 'military' Christmas in millions of homes. And here's a 'military' idea for your Christmas baking."—Gold Medal Flour advertisement with cookie patterns of a pursuit plane, tank, bomb, field gun, battleship, sailor, etc. to trace, December 1942

WARTIME SPECIAL

Coconut or Nut Fingers

Billed as "Bread into Cake" this sweetened condensed milk recipe converts day-old bread into a sweet, cookie-like snack.

½ loaf firm, unsliced, day-old white bread

¾ cup sweetened condensed milk

1 cup flaked coconut or chopped nuts

Preheat oven to 350°F. Grease a baking sheet. Remove crusts from bread and cut bread into four ¾-inch thick slices. Quarter each slice to make a total of 16 fingers. Pour milk into a shallow bowl and spread out coconut or nuts on a piece of waxed paper. Dip bread fingers into milk, rolling to coat all sides, then roll in coconut or nuts and place on baking sheet.

Bake fingers on top shelf of oven until lightly browned, about 15 minutes. Serve hot or cold.

Makes 16

"From the tiny tots to the grandparents, everybody likes cookies, and in good cookies there is a lot of good food value and nourishment."—*The Book of Cookies*, 1940

5

★ ★ ★ No Time For Failures ★ ★ ★

QUICK BREADS

Basic Muffins	*Orange Marmalade Bread*
Tearoom Muffins	*Quick Cheese Bread*
Applesauce Muffins	*Raisin-Nut Quick Bread*
Corn Muffins	*Soy Victory Mix*
Upside-Down Muffins	*Cornmeal Crisps*
Banana Bread	*Popovers*
Boston Brown Bread	*Southern Spoon Bread*
Fig Bread	*Sticky Buns in a Hurry*
Flaky Sandwich Bread	

WARTIME SPECIAL

Bacon Muffins

WHEN TIME WAS SCARCE, quick breads (those leavened with baking powder or the combination of baking soda and an acid) were the order of the day. Although most pre-war households regularly had biscuits, muffins, popovers, and tea loaves on the menu, their importance increased when the family baker was working away from the home and couldn't wait for yeast breads to rise. To make the process even faster, many recipes called for biscuit mix as a head start. Commercial biscuit mix was available, already contained the necessary shortening, and could be adapted to produce a large variety of baked goods. In addition, magazines created recipes for easy-to-make basic mixes that could be kept on hand for busy times. One of my favorites, which I continued to make well into the 1960s, was simply a combination of self-rising flour and vegetable shortening.

Because sugar and shortening make quick breads tender and give them a longer shelf life, the breads that were designed to be low in those rationed ingredients tended to become dry and were best used within a day of baking. However, bakers soon learned that the addition of applesauce or dried fruit puree kept the breads moist and tender and added flavor. This practical bit of food science was rediscovered in the 1990s when bakers wanted to reduce the amount of fat in their muffins and loaves.

In addition to baking without a rising time, quick breads are easy to make, rarely fail, and offer big flavor for minimal expense. These qualities made them perfect for new bakers. Government programs and magazine articles encouraged home-front cooks to involve the rest of the family in food preparation and quick bread recipes were recommended for boys and girls, pre-teen and older, to bake when they came home from school to be served for the family dinner. Another government theme was avoiding waste. Homemakers were warned about the loss of time, money, and ration coupons when a baked product was unsuccessful and couldn't be used. Quick breads were promoted as a safeguard against that failure and the waste it could cause.

★ ★ ★ ★ ★ ★ ★ Basic Muffins ★ ★ ★ ★ ★ ★ ★

An article in the April 1941 Woman's Home Companion *taught homemakers two methods for making muffins and how to vary them with whatever they had on hand. This recipe uses the muffin method, in which the dry ingredients are combined in a bowl and the liquid ingredients are stirred in just until the flour has been moistened. It produces heartier muffins with a coarser texture than those made with the cake method.*

2 cups unsifted all-purpose flour

2 tablespoons sugar

4 teaspoons baking powder

1/2 teaspoon salt

1 cup milk

1 large egg, lightly beaten

1/4 cup melted vegetable shortening
   or vegetable oil

1/3 cup optional stir-in such as dark
   seedless raisins, chopped dates,
   chopped nuts, chopped candied
   cherries or pineapple, sautéed
   onion, or corn kernels

Heat oven to 400°F. Grease a 12-cup muffin pan. Combine flour, sugar, baking powder, and salt in a medium bowl. Beat together milk, egg, and shortening in a small bowl.

Make a well in the center of the dry ingredients and add the milk mixture. Stir just until all dry ingredients have been moistened. Do not overbeat. Fold in optional stir-in, if desired.

Divide muffin mixture into greased muffin cups and bake 20 to 25 minutes or until a toothpick inserted in the center of one comes out clean.

Cool in pan 5 minutes. Remove to serving container and serve warm.

12 Servings

★ ★ ★ ★ ★ ★ Tearoom Muffins ★ ★ ★ ★ ★ ★

Reminiscent of the "dainty" fare served in ladies' tearooms during the first half of the twentieth century, these muffins are made using the cake method. It calls for whipping the shortening, sugar, and eggs first and then adding the dry ingredients and milk to produce special-occasion muffins with a finer texture, more like cupcakes. This recipe uses a minimal amount of sugar, but prewar versions often included twice as much sugar, or more.

2 cups unsifted all-purpose flour

4 teaspoons baking powder

1/2 teaspoon salt

1/3 cup vegetable shortening or
   softened butter (or a mixture)

1/4 cup sugar

1 large egg

1 cup milk

1 tablespoon grated orange or lemon
   peel, or 1 teaspoon ground
   cinnamon, or ground ginger, or
   vanilla extract, optional

Heat oven to 400°F. Grease a 12-cup muffin pan. Combine flour, baking powder, and salt in a small bowl; set aside.

Beat shortening and sugar in a medium bowl until light and fluffy. Add egg and beat until combined. Very gradually fold in dry ingredients and milk. Add the optional flavoring, if using; stir just until combined. Do not overbeat.

Divide muffin mixture into greased muffin cups and bake 20 to 25 minutes or until a toothpick inserted in the center of one comes out clean.

Cool in pan 5 minutes. Remove to serving container and serve warm.

12 Servings

★ ★ ★ ★ ★ ★ Applesauce Muffins ★ ★ ★ ★ ★ ★

In this recipe the basic muffin batter is low in fat and sugar while the moist, sweet applesauce filling does double duty by providing flavor as well as the sweetness and tenderness that those rationed ingredients would have provided.

2 cups unsifted all-purpose flour

4 teaspoons baking powder

2 teaspoons sugar

½ teaspoon salt

1 cup milk

1 large egg, lightly beaten

2 tablespoons melted vegetable
shortening or vegetable oil

⅔ cup sweetened applesauce

Heat oven to 400°F. Grease a 12-cup muffin pan.

Combine flour, baking powder, sugar, and salt in a medium bowl. Beat together milk, egg, and shortening in a small bowl.

Make a well in the center of the dry ingredients. Add the milk mixture and stir just until dry ingredients have been moistened. Do not overbeat.

Spoon half of muffin batter into greased muffin cups, top with the applesauce and remaining batter. Bake muffins 20 to 25 minutes or until a toothpick inserted in the center of one comes out clean.

Cool in pan 5 minutes. Remove to serving container and serve warm.

12 Servings

★ ★ ★ ★ ★ ★ ★ Corn Muffins ★ ★ ★ ★ ★ ★ ★

This generous recipe was designed for a dinner party in which everyone helped to cook a simple meal that included few rationed foods and lots of fun. Cooking together provided the evening's entertainment as well as dinner.

1²/₃ cups unsifted all-purpose flour

1¹/₃ cups yellow cornmeal

3 tablespoons sugar

4 teaspoons baking powder

³/₄ teaspoon salt

1²/₃ cups milk

2 large eggs, lightly beaten

¹/₃ cup melted vegetable shortening
   or vegetable oil

Heat oven to 400°F. Grease 16 muffin cups or use paper liners.

Combine flour, cornmeal, sugar, baking powder, and salt in a large bowl. Make a well in the center of the dry ingredients. Add the milk, eggs, and shortening. Stir just until all dry ingredients have been moistened. Do not overbeat.

Divide muffin mixture into greased muffin cups and bake 20 to 25 minutes or until a toothpick inserted in the center of one comes out clean.

Cool in pans 5 minutes. Remove to serving container and serve warm.

16 Servings

"Unless you are a culinary artist and don't mind taking risks, follow recipes exactly and use accurate measurements."—*Cook's Away,* 1943

★ ★ ★ ★ ★ Upside-Down Muffins ★ ★ ★ ★ ★

Bran muffin recipes appeared frequently in wartime magazines and cookbooks because they were considered nutritious. This recipe from a 1944 bran advertisement adds excitement to the usual recipe by inverting the muffins to reveal a topping of fresh fruit. The headline announces, "Here's a bran muffin that tastes like cake!"

1 cup unprocessed wheat bran

1 cup milk

1 cup pitted fresh sweet cherries, berries, or sliced peaches

¼ cup honey

¼ cup sugar

3 tablespoons vegetable shortening or softened butter (or a mixture)

1 large egg, lightly beaten

1 cup unsifted all-purpose flour

4 teaspoons baking powder

½ teaspoon salt

Heat oven to 400°F. Combine bran and milk in a small bowl; set aside 5 minutes. Generously grease a 12-cup muffin pan. Divide cherries and honey into cups.

Beat sugar and shortening in a large bowl until light and fluffy. Add egg and beat until combined. Fold in bran mixture, flour, baking powder, and salt just until combined. Do not overbeat.

Divide muffin mixture onto cherries in muffin cups and bake 20 to 25 minutes or until a toothpick inserted in the center of one comes out clean.

Cool in pan 5 minutes. Loosen edges of muffins. Invert muffins onto wire rack; transfer to serving platter and serve warm.

12 Servings

★ ★ ★ ★ ★ ★ ★ Banana Bread ★ ★ ★ ★ ★ ★ ★

Government warnings about waste made it a real necessity to use up those bananas that would soon be overripe. Prewar recipes were likely to include as much as 1 cup of sugar in this American favorite, but wartime recipes immediately took advantage of the fact that ripe bananas can add a lot of sweetness on their own, and the moisture they provide makes it possible to use less shortening as well.

2 cups unsifted all-purpose flour

1 teaspoon baking soda

½ teaspoon salt

⅓ cup vegetable shortening or
   softened butter (or a mixture)

¼ cup packed light brown sugar

1 large egg

1¼ cups mashed ripe banana

½ cup chopped nuts

Preheat oven to 350°F. Grease an 8-inch loaf pan. Combine flour, soda, and salt in a small bowl.

Beat shortening, brown sugar, and egg in a medium bowl with an electric mixer on high speed until fluffy. Add dry ingredients and banana; beat on low speed just until combined. Do not beat until smooth. Stir in nuts. Transfer batter to greased loaf pan.

Bake 45 to 50 minutes or until a toothpick inserted in the center comes out clean.

Cool to room temperature and serve or pack in an airtight container and store in the refrigerator.

10 Servings

★ ★ ★ ★ ★ Boston Brown Bread ★ ★ ★ ★ ★

At a time when factory shifts worked around the clock, seven days a week, and home cooks had to find both the time and ingredients to provide meals their families would like, Boston's traditional Saturday-night supper of baked beans and brown bread became popular all over the country. These moist, molasses-flavored loaves, which can be baked as well as steamed, could be set into a low-temperature oven with the beans and forgotten while the busy cook tackled other problems.

1 cup unsifted all-purpose flour	¼ teaspoon salt
1 cup whole wheat flour	2 cups buttermilk
1 cup cornmeal	⅔ cup dark molasses
2 teaspoons baking soda	½ cup raisins or currants

Preheat oven to 300°F. Grease two 7-inch loaf pans or two 32-ounce tins or pudding molds. Combine all-purpose flour, whole wheat flour, cornmeal, soda, and salt in a medium bowl.

Stir together buttermilk and molasses in a large bowl. Add dry ingredients and stir just until they are moistened. Don't overbeat. Fold in raisins. Divide batter between greased loaf pans or molds and bake 55 to 60 minutes (or cover tightly and steam 1½ hours) until a toothpick inserted in the centers comes out clean.

Cool 15 minutes in pans or molds; invert, slice and serve or cool to room temperature, pack in an airtight container, and store in the refrigerator.

20 Servings

★ ★ ★ ★ ★ ★ ★ ★ Fig Bread ★ ★ ★ ★ ★ ★ ★ ★

Dried fruit is much more tender these days than it was in the 1940s, so the figs only need a brief soaking to rehydrate them for this recipe. Steaming directions are included because during the war many families lived in shared housing in order to be near their workplaces. They frequently had no ovens and often their kitchens were a single hot plate in the corner of a bedroom. Steaming breads such as this one, and also cakes, was a way that they could still make these treats for their families.

1 pound dried figs, stems removed

½ cup boiling water

1 cup yellow cornmeal

1 cup whole wheat flour

1 cup unsifted all-purpose flour

1½ teaspoons baking soda

½ teaspoon salt

1½ cups buttermilk

½ cup light molasses

1 large egg, beaten

Quarter figs and combine with water in a small bowl; set aside 15 minutes.

Meanwhile, grease two 8-inch loaf pans. Combine cornmeal, flours, soda, and salt in a large bowl. Preheat oven to 350°F.

Add buttermilk, molasses, and egg to the dry ingredients and stir just until combined. Do not beat until smooth. Fold in figs and any liquid remaining in bowl. Divide mixture between greased loaf pans.

Bake 45 to 50 minutes or until a toothpick inserted in the center comes out clean.

Cool to room temperature and serve or pack in an airtight container.

16 Servings

★ ★ ★ ★ ★ Flaky Sandwich Bread ★ ★ ★ ★ ★

America's farms produced an abundance of grain during World War II, and grain-based products like cereals were considered a nutritious addition to all sorts of baked products. Toasted cereal flakes give added flavor to this everyday sandwich bread.

1¾ cups unsifted all-purpose flour

1 cup flaked whole grain cereal

¼ cup packed light brown sugar

4 teaspoons baking powder

½ teaspoon salt

¾ cup milk

1 large egg

3 tablespoons light molasses

3 tablespoons vegetable shortening
  or butter (or a mixture), melted

Preheat oven to 350°F. Grease an 8-inch loaf pan.

Combine flour, cereal, brown sugar, baking powder, and salt in a large bowl. Beat together milk, egg, molasses, and shortening in a small bowl.

Add milk mixture to dry ingredients and stir just until dry ingredients are moistened. Don't overbeat. Transfer to greased loaf pan.

Bake 45 to 50 minutes or until a toothpick inserted in the center comes out clean.

Cool to room temperature; wrap tightly and refrigerate several hours before slicing.

10 Servings

★ ★ ★ ★ Orange Marmalade Bread ★ ★ ★ ★

Orange marmalade provides big flavor and a bit of sweetness in this easy bread. The little fat that it contains comes from the half-and-half.

2½ cups unsifted all-purpose flour

¼ cup packed light brown sugar

4 teaspoons baking powder

½ teaspoon salt

1 cup half-and-half

¾ cup orange marmalade

1 large egg

½ cup chopped nuts, optional

Preheat oven to 350°F. Grease an 8-inch loaf pan. Stir together flour, brown sugar, baking powder, and salt in a large bowl. Add half-and-half, marmalade, and egg to dry ingredients and stir just until combined. Do not beat until smooth. Stir in nuts, if desired. Transfer batter to greased loaf pan.

Bake 45 to 50 minutes or until a toothpick inserted in the center comes out clean.

Cool to room temperature and serve, or pack in an airtight container.

12 Servings

"When Grandma wanted to truly elate us,
She'd mix sour milk with saleratus*
To leaven the batter for muffin or cake
Whose rival in heaven the angels might bake;
Her quick breads were famous for texture
    and lightness
No cook 'round about could challenge their rightness."
—*Food . . . As We Like It*, 1943

*Saleratus was a base, such as baking soda, that was combined with an acid for leavening.

★ ★ ★ ★ ★ ★ Quick Cheese Bread ★ ★ ★ ★ ★ ★

This recipe must have called for "American Cheddar" out of patriotism because imported Cheddar was not available. It is important to use natural Cheddar rather than processed American cheese, which tends to disappear into the batter.

1³/₄ cups unsifted all-purpose flour

1 cup shredded cheddar cheese

4 teaspoons baking powder

1 teaspoon sugar

³/₄ teaspoon salt

³/₄ cup milk

2 large eggs, beaten

3 tablespoons vegetable shortening
    or butter (or a mixture), melted

Preheat oven to 350°F. Grease an 8-inch loaf pan. Combine flour, ³/₄ cup cheese, baking powder, sugar, and salt in a large bowl. Add milk, eggs, and shortening to dry ingredients and stir just until combined. Do not beat until smooth. Transfer batter to greased loaf pan; sprinkle with remaining ¹/₄ cup cheese.

Bake 50 to 55 minutes or until a toothpick inserted in the center comes out clean.

Cool to room temperature and serve, or pack in an airtight container.

12 Servings

 The December 1943 issue of *Better Homes & Gardens* suggested that busy cooks stack pancakes seven high and cut into wedges to serve for dessert.

★ ★ ★ ★ ★ Raisin-Nut Quick Bread ★ ★ ★ ★ ★

The raisins in this recipe were originally soaked several hours or overnight because they were dryer than our raisins today. For a more festive version of this loaf, substitute chopped mixed dried fruit for the raisins.

1 cup raisins	1 cup milk
2¼ cups unsifted all-purpose flour	1 large egg, beaten
½ cup packed light brown sugar	2 tablespoons vegetable shortening
4 teaspoons baking powder	or butter (or a mixture), melted
½ teaspoon salt	1 cup chopped nuts

Preheat oven to 350°F. Grease a 9-inch loaf pan. Cover raisins with water in a small bowl; set aside 5 minutes, then drain.

Meanwhile, combine flour, brown sugar, baking powder, and salt in a large bowl. Add milk, egg, and shortening to dry ingredients and stir just until combined. Do not beat until smooth. Stir in raisins and nuts. Transfer batter to greased loaf pan.

Bake 45 to 50 minutes or until a toothpick inserted in the center comes out clean.

Cool to room temperature and serve, or pack in an airtight container.

12 Servings

 "Save Fresh Fluid milk.... Rinse cream bottles with milk, and use with milk; rinse milk bottles with water, and use in cooking."—*Your Share*, 1943

★ ★ ★ ★ ★ ★ ★ Soy Victory Mix ★ ★ ★ ★ ★ ★ ★

An article in the January 1943 Farm Journal, *called "The Spotlight's on Soys," told homemakers, "Soybeans are taking a bow these days in the wartime food show." The government promoted the use of soy during the war as a protein supplement. Soy flour was added to many baked products, and soybeans were incorporated into soups, stews, and meat loaves. The recipe that follows can be used to make 4 batches of biscuits or muffins, or 2 nut breads and one of the other recipes.*

6 cups unsifted all-purpose flour	3 teaspoons salt
2 cups unsifted soy flour	1¼ cups lard or vegetable shortening
4 tablespoons baking powder	

Combine all-purpose flour, soy flour, baking powder, and salt in a large bowl. Cut lard into dry ingredients with pastry blender or two knives used scissors fashion until mixture is the consistency of coarse crumbs. Store in a tightly closed container in the refrigerator and use in any of the following recipes.

Biscuits: Preheat oven to 450°F. Grease a baking sheet. To **2 cups of mix**, add ⅔ **cup milk.** Roll out and cut into 12 small biscuits. Place on greased baking sheet and bake until golden and firm to the touch, about 12 minutes.

Scones: Prepare biscuit recipe above adding ¼ **cup raisins** and **2 tablespoons sugar** to the mix. Pat into a 12-inch square. Cut into four 6-inch squares; cut each square diagonally in half to make a total of 8 scones. Bake as directed above.

Muffins: Preheat oven to 400°F. Grease a 12-cup muffin pan. Combine **2 cups mix,** ¾ **cup milk, 1 egg,** and **3 tablespoons sugar** in a medium bowl and stir just until dry ingredients are moistened. Divide batter into greased muffin cups and bake until golden and firm to the touch, 20 to 25 minutes.

Nut Bread: Preheat oven to 350°F. Grease a 9-inch loaf pan. Combine **3 cups mix, 1 cup milk, 1/2 cup chopped nuts, 1 egg,** and **3 tablespoons honey** in a large bowl and stir just until dry ingredients are moistened. Transfer batter to greased loaf pan and bake until golden and firm to the touch, 55 to 60 minutes.

8 Cups Mix

 "Have you ever wished you were blessed with 'a born knack for baking?' Stop your wishing! There's no such thing to be had! Baking skill is made not born."—*All About Home Baking*, 1937

★ ★ ★ ★ ★ ★ Cornmeal Crisps ★ ★ ★ ★ ★ ★

Wartime American farmers responded enthusiastically to government encouragement to produce an abundance of grains for use at home and to share with our allies overseas. At the same time, government-sponsored advertising and public-relations programs encouraged bakers to use grains in new and creative ways. These crunchy cornmeal crackers seem like something you would find in the top restaurants today. It was suggested that they be served with soups or salads.

1 cup cornmeal

½ cup unsifted all-purpose flour

¼ teaspoon salt

¼ teaspoon baking soda

⅓ to ½ cup milk

3 tablespoons margarine or butter

(or a mixture), melted

Preheat oven to 350°F. Grease 2 large baking sheets. Combine cornmeal, flour, salt, and soda in a large bowl. Stir in ⅓ cup milk and the margarine. Stir with a fork until a stiff dough forms, adding more milk, if necessary. Knead dough until smooth, about 5 minutes.

Divide dough into 36 balls. Flatten balls into 2½-inch rounds and place as many as possible ½ inch apart on greased baking sheets. Bake until crisp and beginning to brown, 10 to 12 minutes. Remove to wire racks to cool.

36 Crackers

" 'Fondly Yours' are tiny hot muffins rolled quick as a flash in melted butter or margarine, then in crushed peppermint candy."—*Woman's Home Companion*, April 1943

★ ★ ★ ★ ★ ★ ★ ★ Popovers ★ ★ ★ ★ ★ ★ ★ ★

When popovers are served, any meal becomes a special event. Requiring few ingredients and simple preparation, popovers were especially well suited to meet the needs of wartime bakers.

1 cup milk	2 large eggs
3/4 cup plus 2 tablespoons unsifted all-purpose flour	1 tablespoon butter, melted, optional
	1/4 teaspoon salt

Heat oven to 450°F. Grease 8 custard cups or muffin cups. If using custard cups set them in a large baking pan for easy handling. Combine milk, flour, eggs, butter, if using, and salt in a medium bowl. Beat with an electric mixer on low speed until smooth, scraping bowl frequently. Divide batter into greased cups.

Bake popovers 20 minutes; reduce oven temperature to 350°F and bake 20 minutes longer. Pierce side of each popover with the tip of a knife and bake 5 to 10 minutes longer or until golden and crisp.

Turn out of cups immediately and serve hot.

8 Servings

"Avoid failures by using this flour and Betty Crocker recipes. *Cut down on kitchen waste.* All Gold Medal is vitamin and mineral enriched. Thus it's a 'preferred' food."
—Gold Medal Flour advertisement, 1942

★ ★ ★ ★ ★ Southern Spoon Bread ★ ★ ★ ★ ★

The note that accompanied this recipe in a 1943 community cookbook said that the homemaker who contributed the recipe served it as a main dish in place of meat, along with a salad and green vegetable. I recommend substituting a cup of corn kernels in place of the coconut, when you want a change.

1 cup yellow cornmeal

1 cup cold water

1 cup boiling water

1 teaspoon salt

1 cup milk

2 large eggs, well beaten

1 tablespoon butter, melted

1 cup shredded coconut or yellow
  corn kernels

Preheat oven to 400°F. Grease a 1½-quart shallow baking dish. Combine cornmeal and cold water in a medium saucepan; beat in boiling water and salt. Cook over medium heat, stirring until thickened. Combine milk, eggs, and butter; beat into cornmeal mixture along with coconut or corn.

Transfer pudding to greased baking dish and bake 25 to 30 minutes.

Cool slightly and serve from baking dish.

6 to 8 Servings

"The backbone of a nation is the good housekeeper, and the home makers' greatest asset is the ability to prepare good food." —*Hamilton Ross Modern Cook Book*, 1940

★ ★ ★ ★ ★ Sticky Buns in a Hurry ★ ★ ★ ★ ★

Using biscuit dough rather than yeast dough makes it possible to turn out a batch of sticky buns in under an hour—a special treat for a busy day and a boon to busy wartime cooks. These can even serve as a dessert when accompanied by fresh fruit or ice cream.

2 cups unsifted all-purpose flour	2 tablespoons butter, melted
4 teaspoons baking powder	3/4 cup packed light brown sugar
1/2 teaspoon salt	1/2 teaspoon ground cinnamon
1/4 cup vegetable shortening	1/2 cup light corn syrup
1/2 cup milk	1/2 cup nuts or raisins, optional
1 large egg, lightly beaten	

Heat oven to 400°F. Grease a 9-inch square baking pan. Combine flour, baking powder, and salt in a medium bowl. Cut in shortening with a pastry blender or two knives until the mixture forms coarse crumbs. Beat together milk and egg in a small bowl; add milk mixture to dry ingredients and stir just until all dry ingredients have been moistened.

Turn mixture out onto a floured work surface and roll out to a 12- by 9-inch rectangle. Spread 1 tablespoon of melted butter over surface of dough. Sprinkle with 1/2 cup brown sugar and 1/4 teaspoon cinnamon. Roll up to make a 9-inch log; slice crosswise into 9 rounds.

Drizzle remaining 1 tablespoon butter over bottom of greased baking pan; sprinkle with remaining 1/4 cup brown sugar and 1/4 teaspoon cinnamon. Drizzle with corn syrup and add nuts or raisins, if using. Arrange dough rounds in pan with a cut side up.

Bake 20 to 25 minutes or until buns have browned and feel firm when one in the center of the pan is gently pressed with a spoon. Loosen edges and invert onto serving plate; serve warm.

9 Servings

WARTIME SPECIAL

Bacon Muffins

A container of bacon fat was a staple in most 1940s American iceboxes. Saved from cooking bacon for many breakfasts, the fat was used to season vegetables, to sauté fritters and breaded meats, and sometimes for baking. In this recipe, the bacon fat provides the shortening and maple syrup provides the sweetness. Serve these savory muffins with a Victory Garden all-vegetable meal and they will add a touch of meat to the menu.

6 slices bacon, cut into 1-inch pieces
2 cups unsifted all-purpose flour
4 teaspoons baking powder
1/4 teaspoon salt
1 cup milk

1 large egg, lightly beaten
1/4 cup warm bacon fat
   (from cooking bacon)
2 tablespoons maple syrup

Cook bacon in a large skillet over medium heat, stirring frequently. Remove bacon to paper towels to drain; reserve bacon fat. Heat oven to 400°F. Grease a 12-cup muffin pan.

Combine flour, bacon pieces, baking powder, and salt in a medium bowl. Beat together milk, egg, bacon fat, and maple syrup in a small bowl.

Make a well in the center of the dry ingredients. Add the milk mixture. Stir just until all dry ingredients have been moistened. Do not overbeat.

Divide muffin mixture into greased muffin cups and bake 20 to 25 minutes or until a toothpick inserted in the center of one comes out clean.

Cool in pan 5 minutes. Remove to serving container and serve warm.

12 Servings

6

★ ★ ★ Rising to the Occasion ★ ★ ★

YEAST BREADS

American Rye Bread

Anadama Bread

Basic White Bread

Breakfast Cake

Easy Coffee Ring

English Tea Cake

Holiday Coffee Bread

Lemon Cheese Buns

Mrs. Nesbitt's Whole Wheat Bread

No-Knead Refrigerator Rolls

Oatmeal Bread

Potato Bread

Sugarplum Loaf

Victory Rolls

WARTIME SPECIAL

Celery Horns

COST OF LIVING

1918

64.6% RISE IN COST OF LIVING 53RD MONTH WORLD WAR I

1944

COST OF LIVING

Price Control Began Here

Before Price Control

RISE IN COST OF LIVING 53RD MONTH WORLD WAR II **25.9%**

Here's a war job all America may be proud of. The rise in the wartime cost of living today is less than half the World War I increase... only the patriotic cooperation of the public and businessmen with the government's price control program made this record possible... let's keep up the good work by keeping the **Home Front Pledge:**

"I pay no more than ceiling prices.. ..I pay my ration points in full."

UNITED STATES OFFICE OF PRICE ADMINISTRATION

A 1942 PAMPHLET BY Fleischmann's Home Economics Department discouragingly notes, "Baking Day isn't on the American housewife's calendar any more." It then goes on to add, "But there are times when women like to run up a batch of rolls of their own, or try their hand at a coffee cake, just to see if they can still do it!" When the war started homemade yeast bread was still on most tables occasionally, if not every day. As more and more women began to work away from the home, yeast bread making was one of the first casualties. In an effort to encourage bakers to return to yeast breads, magazines ran stories frequently promoting homemade bread as a special treat, or a morale booster. A May 1942 *Woman's Home Companion* article suggested that a loaf of homemade bread with butter and coffee was the most impressive party refreshment that could be served to friends. In addition to enjoying the rate treat of rationed butter and coffee, guests would feel honored that the hostess had taken time from her busy schedule to bake homemade bread for them. Magazine articles on holiday meals still regularly included a recipe for a special homemade bread.

As the war continued, recipes that called for conveniently raising breads in the refrigerator, along with longer lines to purchase bread in supermarkets and bakeries, made home baking more attractive. Homemakers began to realize that yeast breads offered a big value for the least possible expenditure of sugar and shortening. Low-fat, low-sugar, yeast-raised buns and coffee cakes started to appear on the menu as dessert. The recipes that follow have all been converted from the fresh yeast cakes that were used during the war to active dry yeast, which is more easily found these days. Interestingly, fresh yeast cakes were not only used for baking but were considered a vitamin supplement. One of my favorite wartime snacks was fresh yeast spread on graham crackers with peanut butter. It had been prescribed to my mother by our family physician, and she always shared her vitamins with me.

★ ★ ★ ★ ★ American Rye Bread ★ ★ ★ ★ ★

These loaves are American in that they are less dense than the traditional European rye bread. But also, it didn't hurt to emphasize the fact that this recipe had nothing to do with the bread favored by the enemy.

1 cup milk	2 packages (2¼ teaspoons each)
2 tablespoons light molasses	active dry yeast
1 tablespoon vegetable shortening or	4 cups rye flour
butter (or a mixture)	2 cups unsifted all-purpose flour
1 teaspoon salt	2 teaspoons white vinegar
³/₄ cup warm (105° to 110°F) water	2 teaspoons caraway seeds, optional

Heat milk in a small saucepan over medium heat until bubbles form at edge of pan; stir in molasses, shortening, and salt. Transfer to a large bowl and set aside to cool to 105° to 110°F. Combine warm water and yeast in a cup and set aside for yeast to soften.

When milk mixture has cooled, add 2 cups rye flour, the all-purpose flour, yeast mixture, vinegar, and caraway seeds, if using; stir until a soft dough forms. Stir in 1 to 1½ cups of remaining rye flour until dough is manageable. Turn dough out onto a work surface floured with some of remaining rye flour. Knead 5 minutes, adding as much of the flour as necessary to make the dough manageable. Place dough in a greased bowl, cover and set aside in a warm place until double in size—about 1 hour.

Grease two 8-inch loaf pans. Divide dough in half, shape each half into a log and fit into one of the greased pans. Set aside in a warm place until double in size—about 45 minutes.

Preheat oven to 350°F. Brush tops of loaves with water. Bake bread 35 to 40 minutes, or until loaves sound hollow when tapped on the top.

Cool at least 30 minutes before slicing.

20 Servings

★ ★ ★ ★ ★ ★ Anadama Bread ★ ★ ★ ★ ★ ★

Surprisingly, the recipe for this traditional bread met the needs of wartime bakers by being "sugarless," low in shortening, and easy to assemble—and the familiar aroma of the bread baking has given New England families comfort for many generations. The story behind the unusual name is that a fisherman who was tired of being served cornmeal mush and molasses for dinner each evening combined the ingredients to make a delicious bread. Cursing his wife for her laziness, "Anna, damn her," he named the bread.

1 cup yellow cornmeal

1/3 cup light molasses

3 tablespoons vegetable shortening
   or butter (or a mixture)

1 1/2 teaspoons salt

1 1/4 cups boiling water

1 package (2 1/4 teaspoons) active dry
   yeast

3 1/2 to 4 cups unsifted all-purpose
   flour

Measure cornmeal, molasses, shortening, and salt into a large bowl. Gradually stir boiling water into the mixture until the shortening melts and the molasses dissolves. Set aside until the mixture cools to between 105° and 110°F.

When mixture has cooled, sprinkle yeast over surface and set aside to allow yeast to soften, about 5 minutes. Then, stir in 3 to 3 1/2 cups flour until a soft dough forms. Turn dough out onto a work surface floured with some of the remaining flour. Knead 5 minutes, adding as much of the flour as necessary to make the dough manageable. Shape dough into a ball, place in a greased bowl, cover loosely, and set aside in a warm place until double in size—about 1 hour. Meanwhile, grease a 9-inch loaf pan.

Punch dough down; shape into a log and place in the greased pan. Cover loosely and set aside in a warm place until 1 inch above top of pan—about 45 minutes.

Preheat oven to 375°F. Bake loaf 35 to 40 minutes or until golden brown and it sounds hollow when tapped on the top. Loosen edges and remove to cooling rack.

Cool at least 20 minutes before slicing.

12 Servings

★ ★ ★ ★ ★ ★ Basic White Bread ★ ★ ★ ★ ★ ★

Wartime homemakers were of a generation used to the concept of bread being made in the home. Even for young homemakers just starting out, learning to make their own bread was easier than standing in line at the grocer's or baker's to get it already made. Although the recipe sounds as if it takes a long time, most of it is just rising and baking time; the baker can do other things while these processes take care of themselves.

1 cup milk
3 tablespoons sugar
2 tablespoons vegetable shortening
  or butter (or a mixture)
1½ teaspoons salt

1 cup warm (105° to 110°F) water
2 packages (2¼ teaspoons each)
  active dry yeast
6 to 6½ cups unsifted all-purpose
  flour

Heat milk in a small saucepan over medium heat until bubbles form at edge of pan; stir in sugar, shortening, and salt. Transfer to a large bowl and set aside to cool to 105° to 110°F. Combine warm water and yeast in a cup and set aside for yeast to soften.

When milk mixture has cooled, add 6 cups flour and the yeast mixture; stir until a soft dough forms. Turn dough out onto a work surface floured with some of remaining ½ cup flour. Knead 5 minutes, adding as much of the flour as necessary to make the dough manageable. Place dough in a greased bowl, cover, and set aside in a warm place until double in size—about 1 hour.

Grease two 8-inch loaf pans. Divide dough in half and shape into 2 logs; fit into the greased pans. Set aside in a warm place until dough has risen at least 1 inch above sides of pans—about 45 minutes.

Preheat oven to 375°F. Bake breads 35 to 40 minutes, or until golden brown and loaves sound hollow when tapped on the top.

Cool at least 30 minutes before slicing.

VARIATIONS

Raisin Bread: Add ½ cup dark seedless raisins to the milk mixture before adding the flour.

Cheddar Bread: Mix 1 cup coarsely grated cheddar cheese into the first 2 cups of flour that are stirred into the cooled milk mixture. Sprinkle tops of loaves with additional cheese, if desired.

Cinnamon Swirl Bread: Roll out each half of dough to a 12- by 8-inch rectangle. Combine ¼ cup sugar and 2 teaspoons ground cinnamon. Sprinkle half over each piece of dough; roll up dough to make two 8-inch logs.

24 Servings

 "Because bread is high in food energy doesn't mean it will produce overweight. The control of weight depends on the food energy of all the foods you eat and not on any one specific food."—*The Bread Basket,* 1942

★ ★ ★ ★ ★ ★ Breakfast Cake ★ ★ ★ ★ ★ ★

It is amazing how many tempting sweets can be made from this basic dough. My grandmother-in-law used to make it frequently, incorporating whatever fruit was in season. If it was the middle of the winter, she used homemade jam, rehydrated dried fruit, or just a streusel topping.

1 cup milk

$\frac{1}{3}$ cup sugar

$\frac{1}{4}$ cup vegetable shortening or
  butter (or a mixture)

$\frac{3}{4}$ teaspoon salt

$\frac{1}{3}$ cup warm (105° to 110°F) water

2 packages ($2\frac{1}{4}$ teaspoons each)
  active dry yeast

$4\frac{1}{2}$ to 5 cups unsifted all-purpose
  flour

1 large egg, lightly beaten

1 large apple or peach, peeled and
  sliced, or $\frac{1}{2}$ cup dried apricots,
  quartered peaches or pears, soaked
  in the refrigerator overnight

1 tablespoon butter, melted

3 tablespoons packed light brown
  sugar

1 teaspoon ground cinnamon

Heat milk in a small saucepan over medium heat until bubbles form at edge of pan; stir in sugar, shortening, and salt. Transfer to a large bowl and set aside to cool to 105° to 110°F. Combine warm water and yeast in a cup and set aside for yeast to soften.

When milk mixture has cooled, add $4\frac{1}{2}$ cups flour, the beaten egg, and the yeast mixture; stir until a soft dough forms. Turn dough out onto a work surface floured with some of remaining $\frac{1}{2}$ cup flour. Knead 5 minutes, adding as much of the flour as necessary to make the dough manageable. Place dough in a greased bowl, cover, and set aside in a warm place until double in size—about 1 hour.

Grease two 9-inch round cake pans. Divide dough in half. Place each half on one of the greased pans and flatten to fill the pan. Cover and set aside in a warm place until double in size—about 45 minutes.

Preheat oven to 350°F. Cut as many slits in dough as you have pieces of fruit. Insert a piece of fruit in each slit; brush with melted butter. Combine brown sugar and cinnamon and sprinkle over breakfast cakes.

Cover and bake 15 minutes; uncover and bake 10 to 15 minutes longer, or until golden brown and cake sounds hollow when tapped on the top.

Cool 10 to 15 minutes; slice and serve.

VARIATIONS

Jam Cake: Press half of each ball of dough into each greased pan. Spread each with ¼ **cup jam** (seedless red raspberry is my favorite). Coarsely chop remaining dough, toss until coated with **1 tablespoon melted butter**, **1 tablespoon packed light brown sugar**, and ½ **teaspoon ground cinnamon**; drop half of mixture on top of each pan. Raise and bake, uncovered, for 25 to 30 minutes.

Streusel Coffee Cake: Combine ¾ cup fresh bread crumbs, ¼ cup packed light brown sugar, and 1 teaspoon ground cinnamon. Stir in 3 tablespoons melted butter. Press "dimples" into raised coffee cakes and sprinkle with streusel mixture. Bake, uncovered, for 25 to 30 minutes.

16 Servings

"Like sugar, whole grain cereals and the accommodating potato are energy foods. One small potato gives the equivalent in quick energy of two tablespoons sugar."—*Woman's Home Companion*, May 1942

★ ★ ★ ★ ★ ★ Easy Coffee Ring ★ ★ ★ ★ ★ ★ ★

Perfect for a busy weekend, this coffee ring can be in the oven in half the time because the soft dough needs only one rising.

¾ cup milk

½ cup packed light brown sugar

¼ cup vegetable shortening or
   butter (or a mixture)

½ teaspoon salt

¼ cup warm (105° to 110°F) water

1 package (2¼ teaspoons) active dry
   yeast

3 to 3½ cups unsifted all-purpose
   flour

1 large egg, lightly beaten

½ cup fresh white bread crumbs

1 tablespoon butter, melted

1 teaspoon ground cinnamon

Heat milk in a small saucepan over medium heat until bubbles form at edge of pan; stir in ¼ cup brown sugar, the shortening, and salt. Transfer to a large bowl and set aside to cool to 105° to 110°F.

Meanwhile, combine warm water and yeast in a cup and set aside for yeast to soften. Grease a 9-inch tube pan; line the bottom with wax paper and grease wax paper.

When milk mixture has cooled, add 3 cups flour, the beaten egg and the yeast mixture; stir until a soft dough forms. Turn dough out onto a work surface floured with some of remaining ½ cup flour. Knead 5 minutes, adding as much of the flour as necessary to make a soft dough. Place dough in prepared tube pan.

Stir together the bread crumbs, remaining ¼ cup brown sugar, the butter, and the cinnamon in a small bowl until combined. Gently spread the mixture over the top of the ring, pressing it onto the surface of the dough. Cover the pan with an oiled sheet of aluminum foil and set it aside in a warm place until double in size—about 1 hour.

Preheat oven to 375° F. Uncover the ring and bake it until the crumb topping is golden brown and the bread sounds hollow when tapped on the top with a kitchen knife (don't use fingers as the topping gets very hot), 30 to 35 minutes.

Cool ring 5 minutes in pan. Loosen bread from edge of pan and center tube. Remove to cooling rack and cool at least 30 minutes before slicing.

10 Servings

"Spread a little Eagle Brand Sweetened Condensed Milk on plain bread, and see how the youngsters go for it. It's good for them, too—helps put a little extra milk into their diet."—*Borden's Eagle Brand Magic Recipes,* 1946

★ ★ ★ ★ ★ ★ English Tea Cake ★ ★ ★ ★ ★ ★ ★

Perfect for breakfast or afternoon tea, this nut-topped coffee cake fills the bill as a low-sugar wartime dessert.

¼ cup evaporated milk or half-and-half

¼ cup vegetable shortening or butter (or a mixture)

¼ cup packed light brown sugar

½ teaspoon salt

¼ cup warm (105° to 110°F) water

1 package (2¼ teaspoons) active dry yeast

1½ cups unsifted all-purpose flour

⅓ cup dried currants

1 large egg, lightly beaten

¼ cup walnuts

½ teaspoon ground cinnamon

Heat milk in a small saucepan over medium heat until bubbles form at edge of pan; stir in shortening, 2 tablespoons brown sugar, and the salt. Transfer to a large bowl and set aside to cool to 105° to 110°F. Meanwhile, combine warm water and yeast in a cup and set aside for yeast to soften.

When milk mixture has cooled, beat in flour, currants, egg, and the yeast mixture; stir until a soft dough forms. Cover bowl and set aside in a warm place to rise slightly—30 minutes.

Meanwhile, grease an 8-inch square baking pan; combine walnuts with remaining 2 tablespoons brown sugar and the cinnamon in a small bowl.

Transfer soft dough to greased pan and smooth top surface. Sprinkle with walnut mixture. Cover and set aside in a warm place to rise slightly—30 minutes.

Preheat oven to 400°F. Bake tea cake until golden brown and it sounds hollow when tapped on the top, 20 to 25 minutes.

Cool 5 minutes in pan; remove to cooling rack and cool 15 to 20 minutes; cut into 9 squares and serve warm.

9 Servings

★ ★ ★ ★ ★ Holiday Coffee Bread ★ ★ ★ ★ ★

This enticing bread appeared in a wartime advertisement for yeast. A special holiday yeast bread has always been a tradition in my home, and the fact that you can produce a spectacular treat with very little sugar and butter must have been very appealing to homemakers who wanted to provide a holiday to remember even in the bleakest of times.

½ cup milk

3 tablespoons vegetable shortening
   or butter (or a mixture)

2 tablespoons sugar

¾ teaspoon salt

¼ cup warm (105° to 110°F) water

1 package (2¼ teaspoons) active dry
   yeast

2¼ to 2¾ cups unsifted all-purpose
   flour

1 large egg, lightly beaten

1 tablespoon packed light brown
   sugar

1 teaspoon grated orange or lemon
   peel

½ teaspoon ground cinnamon

2 tablespoons orange or lemon juice

¼ cup seedless red raspberry jam

Confectioners' Sugar Glaze (recipe
   follows)

Heat milk in a small saucepan over medium heat until bubbles form at edge of pan; stir in shortening, sugar, and salt. Transfer to a large bowl and set aside to cool to 105° to 110°F. Meanwhile, combine warm water and yeast in a cup and set aside for yeast to soften.

When milk mixture has cooled, add 2¼ cups flour, the beaten egg and the yeast mixture; stir until a soft dough forms. Turn dough out onto a work surface floured with some of remaining ½ cup flour. Knead 5 minutes adding as much of the flour as necessary to make the dough manageable. Place dough in a greased bowl, cover and set aside in a warm place until double in size—about 1 hour.

Meanwhile, grease a medium baking sheet and combine brown sugar, orange peel, and cinnamon in a small bowl. Roll out dough on a floured surface with a floured rolling pin to make a 14- by 10-inch rectangle. Brush the surface of the dough with orange juice and sprinkle evenly with brown sugar mixture. Starting at each 10-inch side of rectangle, roll up dough, jelly-roll fashion, to meet in center. Transfer dough to greased baking sheet. With scissors, snip dough rolls at 2-inch intervals to within ½ inch of inner side of rolls. Twist each dough slice to show cut side. Cover loaf loosely with a sheet of wax paper and set aside in a warm place until double in size—about 45 minutes. Spoon preserves down center of loaf.

Preheat oven to 350°F. Bake 25 to 30 minutes, or until golden brown and loaf sounds hollow when tapped on the top.

Cool 15 to 20 minutes, then drizzle with glaze.

Confectioners' Sugar Glaze: Stir together ½ **cup unsifted confectioners' sugar** and **about 2 teaspoons orange or lemon juice** until smooth.

6 Servings

"Niacin is the new name for nicotinic acid, one of the important B vitamins now being added to enriched white bread. Nicotinic acid, alias niacin, has no connection with the nicotine found in tobacco."—*Woman's Home Companion*, May 1942

"Fleischmann's Fresh Yeast in tomato juice is a fine 'Vitamin Cocktail.' It supplies every vitamin known to be needed in human nutrition—the tomato juice adding vitamin C, the only well-known vitamin not supplied by Fleischmann's Yeast."—*The Bread Basket*, 1942

★ ★ ★ ★ ★ ★ Lemon Cheese Buns ★ ★ ★ ★ ★ ★ ★

A simple, low-fat version of cheese Danish, these wartime breakfast rolls feature a filling that is made with eggs and unrationed cottage cheese—both plentiful on the home front because they were too perishable to ship overseas. I have recommended using rimmed baking sheets just in case some of the filling expands out of the buns.

3/4 cup milk

5 tablespoons sugar

1/4 cup melted vegetable shortening
  or oil

1 1/2 teaspoons grated lemon peel

1/2 teaspoon salt

1/4 teaspoon ground mace

1/4 cup warm (105° to 110°F) water

1 package (2 1/4 teaspoons) active dry
  yeast

3 to 3 1/4 cups unsifted all-purpose
  flour

1 cup creamed cottage cheese

1 large egg, lightly beaten

1/4 cup dark seedless raisins

Heat milk in a small saucepan over medium heat until bubbles form at edge of pan; stir in 3 tablespoons sugar, the shortening, 1 teaspoon lemon peel, the salt, and mace. Transfer to a large bowl and set aside to cool to 105° to 110°F. Meanwhile, combine warm water and yeast in a cup and set aside for yeast to soften. Grease 2 rimmed baking sheets.

When milk mixture has cooled, add 3 cups flour and the yeast mixture; stir until a soft dough forms. Turn dough out onto a work surface floured with some of remaining 1/4 cup flour. Knead 5 minutes, adding as much of the flour as necessary to make a soft dough. Divide dough into 12 balls; place on baking sheets and flatten into 3-inch rounds. Cover sheets and set aside in a warm place until double in size—about 1 hour.

When buns have doubled in size, preheat oven to 425°F. Stir together cottage cheese, egg, raisins, remaining 2 tablespoons sugar, and 1/2 teaspoon lemon peel. Press an indentation in the center of each bun with a spoon and divide cheese mixture among them. Bake until golden brown and buns sound hollow when tapped on the side, 15 to 20 minutes.

Remove to cooling rack. Cool 15 to 20 minutes before serving. Store any leftovers in the refrigerator.

24 Servings

"The cook who bakes her bread and rolls
Is everybody's pal;
Just that tantalizing Fragrance
Will help to build morale"
—*Coupon Cookery*, 1943

"One of the commonest mistakes women make in preparing yeast breads is keeping the dough too warm while it is rising. Actually a temperature of 85°F, which may seem cool to you, is more desirable than 90°F. to 95°F."—*Recipes For Good Eating*, 1945

★ ★ Mrs. Nesbitt's Whole Wheat Bread ★ ★

Mrs. Henrietta Nesbitt, White House housekeeper for Franklin and Eleanor Roosevelt, presided over the kitchen with great authority. Although today the quality of the food she served has been questioned, the November 1944 Ladies' Home Journal *article that ran her famous whole wheat bread recipe assured readers that even for important visitors, "meals at the White House are democratic…scarcely more elaborate than your own company dinners—and as distinctly American." Mrs. Nesbitt, of course, made a larger recipe of this bread and used cakes of fresh yeast.*

1½ cups warm (105° to 110°F) water

1 package (2¼ teaspoons) active dry yeast

3 tablespoons light molasses

2 tablespoons vegetable shortening or butter (or a mixture), melted

1 tablespoon packed light brown sugar

1 teaspoon salt

1½ cups whole wheat flour

3 to 3½ cups unsifted all-purpose flour

Combine ½ cup of the warm water and the yeast in a large bowl and set aside for yeast to soften. When yeast has softened, stir in remaining warm water, the molasses, shortening, brown sugar, and salt.

Add whole wheat flour and beat to make a smooth batter. Gradually beat in as much white flour as necessary to make a stiff dough. Place dough in a greased bowl, grease surface of dough, cover and refrigerate overnight.

Next day, grease one 9-inch or two 7-inch loaf pans. Shape dough into 1 or 2 logs; fit into the greased 9-inch or two 7-inch pans. Set aside in a warm place until dough has risen at least 1 inch above sides of pan or pans—about 1 hour.

Preheat oven to 400°F. Bake 15 minutes; reduce oven temperature to 350°F and bake until golden brown and loaf or loaves sound hollow when tapped on the top, 25 to 30 minutes. Cool at least 30 minutes before slicing.

12 to 16 Servings

★ ★ ★ No-Knead Refrigerator Rolls ★ ★ ★

These rolls were advertised as so easy "even a novice should be able to make them successfully." In addition to being easy to assemble, they can be made ahead and raised in the refrigerator.

1¼ cups boiling water

⅓ cup vegetable shortening or
    butter (or a mixture)

2 tablespoons packed light brown
    sugar

1 teaspoon salt

1 package (2¼ teaspoons) active dry
    yeast

1 large egg, lightly beaten

4 to 4½ cups unsifted all-purpose
    flour

1 teaspoon butter, softened

Combine water, shortening, brown sugar, and salt. Pour mixture into a large bowl; set aside to cool to between 105° and 110°F.

When water has cooled, sprinkle yeast over top and set aside 5 minutes for yeast to soften. Beat in egg and 3 cups flour to make a stiff batter. Stir in as much additional flour as necessary to make a soft but manageable dough. Grease a large bowl; shape dough into a ball and place in bowl; cover with a dinner plate and refrigerate 2 to 24 hours.

Grease two 12-cup muffin pans. Divide dough into 24 balls and place in muffin cups. Brush tops with butter; cover loosely and set aside in a warm place until double in size— 1 to 2 hours.

Preheat-oven to 400°F. Bake about 20 minutes or until golden brown and buns sound hollow when tapped on the top. Loosen edges and remove to cooling rack.

Cool at least 20 minutes before serving.

VARIATION

Whole Wheat Rolls: Substitute 1½ cups whole wheat flour for 1½ cups of the all-purpose flour.

24 Servings

★ ★ ★ ★ ★ ★ Oatmeal Bread ★ ★ ★ ★ ★ ★ ★

This recipe provided the nutrition and flavor of oatmeal, reduced the amount of flour necessary to make 2 loaves of bread, and used up some already-cooked cereal that might otherwise have been wasted. It is especially good toasted for breakfast.

½ cup milk	¼ cup warm (105° to 110°F) water
3 tablespoons vegetable shortening or butter (or a mixture)	1 package (2 ¼ teaspoons) active dry yeast
3 tablespoons packed light brown sugar	1 cup cooked oatmeal
1 teaspoon salt	3½ to 4 cups unsifted all-purpose flour

Heat milk in a small saucepan over medium heat until bubbles form at edge of pan; stir in shortening, brown sugar, and salt. Combine warm water and yeast in a cup and set aside for yeast to soften.

Gradually beat hot milk mixture into oatmeal in a large bowl until well blended. Set aside to cool to 105° to 110°F. Add 3½ cups flour and the yeast mixture to the cereal mixture and stir until a soft dough forms. Turn dough out onto a work surface floured with some of remaining ½ cup flour. Knead 5 minutes, adding as much of the flour as necessary to make the dough manageable. Place dough in a greased bowl, cover, and set aside in a warm place until double in size—about 1 hour.

Grease two 8-inch loaf pans. Divide dough into 2 equal pieces. Shape each piece into a ball and place in a greased pan. Set aside in a warm place until double in size—about 45 minutes.

Preheat oven to 400°F. Bake breads 40 to 45 minutes or until golden brown and bread sounds hollow when tapped on the top.

Cool at least 30 minutes before slicing.

24 Servings

★ ★ ★ ★ ★ ★ ★ Potato Bread ★ ★ ★ ★ ★ ★ ★

This frugal recipe produces a firm, moist loaf of bread while using up leftover potatoes in a way that no one will reject. If the mashed potatoes are especially soft, reduce the amount of milk by a tablespoon or two. The bread will stay fresh longer if stored in the refrigerator.

1 cup milk	1/4 cup warm (105° to 110°F) water
1 cup stiff mashed potatoes	1 package (2 1/4 teaspoons) active dry
2 tablespoons sugar	yeast
2 tablespoons vegetable shortening	3 1/2 to 4 1/2 cups unsifted all-purpose
or butter (or a mixture)	flour
3/4 teaspoon salt	1 large egg, lightly beaten

Heat milk in a small saucepan over medium heat until bubbles form at edge of pan; stir in mashed potato, sugar, shortening, and salt. Transfer to a large bowl and set aside to cool to 105° to 110°F. Combine warm water and yeast in a cup and set aside for yeast to soften.

When milk mixture has cooled, add 3 1/2 cups flour, the beaten egg, and the yeast mixture; stir until a soft dough forms. Turn dough out onto a work surface floured with some of remaining 1 cup flour. Knead 5 minutes, adding as much of the flour as necessary to make the dough manageable. Place dough in a greased bowl, cover, and set aside in a warm place until double in size—about 1 hour.

Grease a 9-inch loaf pan. Shape dough into a log and fit into the greased pan. Set aside in a warm place until double in size—about 45 minutes.

Preheat oven to 350°F. Bake bread 40 to 45 minutes, or until golden brown and loaf sounds hollow when tapped on the top.

Cool at least 30 minutes before slicing.

12 Servings

★ ★ ★ ★ ★ ★ Sugarplum Loaf ★ ★ ★ ★ ★ ★ ★

This special-occasion loaf is made using the sponge method, in which only a small amount of flour is added to the dough for the first rising. In this recipe, to take advantage of the fact that sugar increases the action of yeast while salt tends to retard it, the sugar is added to the mixture right away and the salt is not added until after the first rising.

¾ cup warm (105° to 110°F) water

1 package (2¼ teaspoons) active dry yeast

⅓ cup vegetable shortening or softened butter (or a mixture)

⅓ cup sugar

2 large eggs

4 to 4½ cups unsifted all-purpose flour

1 cup mixed candied fruit

½ cup dark seedless raisins

½ cup chopped walnuts, almonds, or pecans

1 teaspoon salt

½ cup unsifted confectioners' sugar

1½ to 2 teaspoons lemon juice

Stir together water and yeast in a small bowl; set aside in a warm place for yeast to soften and rise to the top, about 5 minutes. Generously grease bottom and side of a 9- by 3-inch round baking pan or springform pan.

Beat shortening and sugar until fluffy. Beat in eggs, one at a time. Add 1 cup of the flour and the softened yeast mixture, stirring to make a soft dough. Cover the bowl loosely and set it aside in a warm place until the flour mixture is bubbly and doubles in size—45 minutes to 1 hour.

Stir in 2½ to 3 cups of remaining flour, the candied fruit, raisins, nuts, and salt. Turn dough out onto a work surface floured with some of remaining flour. Knead 5 minutes, adding as much of the flour as necessary to make the dough manageable. Shape dough into a ball, fit into greased pan, cover loosely, and set aside in a warm place until double in size—about 1 hour.

Preheat oven to 375°F. Bake 30 to 35 minutes or until golden brown and loaf sounds hollow when tapped on the top. Loosen edges and remove to cooling rack.

Cool at least 20 minutes before serving.

Meanwhile, combine confectioners' sugar and lemon juice to make a smooth glaze. Drizzle glaze over loaf.

12 Servings

 "Bread today is indeed the 'Staff of Life.' We who know food, and its values, know that there is an enriched loaf of bread behind every man behind every gun!"—*Coupon Cookery,* 1943

★ ★ ★ ★ ★ ★ Victory Rolls ★ ★ ★ ★ ★ ★ ★

Hot cooked cereal was a nutritious part of every home-front warrior's breakfast menu, and so the uncooked toasted wheat cereal was easily available in the cupboard to make the crunchy filling for these rolls.

No-Knead Refrigerator Rolls, whole
   wheat variation (page 130)
⅓ cup toasted wheat cereal,
   uncooked

¼ teaspoon salt
3 tablespoons margarine or butter
   (or a mixture), melted

Prepare roll dough following recipe directions through first rising. Meanwhile, combine cereal and salt in a small bowl. Grease two 9-inch square baking pans.

Roll out dough on a floured surface with a floured rolling pin to make a 14- by-12-inch rectangle. Brush the surface of the dough with melted margarine and sprinkle evenly with ⅔ of the cereal mixture.

Starting at a 12-inch side of the rectangle, roll up dough, jelly roll fashion, to make a 12-inch log. Cut log into 24 slices. Transfer slices to greased baking pans, placing each with a cut side up. Sprinkle remaining cereal mixture over top. Cover loosely and set aside in a warm place to rise until almost double in size, about 45 minutes.

Preheat oven to 400°F. Bake rolls until golden brown and they sound hollow when tapped on the top, about 20 minutes. Loosen edges and remove to cooling rack.

Cool at least 15 minutes before serving.

24 Servings

Celery Horns

These savory crescent rolls are made with easy-to-find, unrationed ingredients and have an unusual celery-seed topping.

½ cup milk	1 package (2¼ teaspoons) active dry
3 tablespoons vegetable shortening	yeast
or butter (or a mixture)	2 cups unsifted all-purpose flour
2 tablespoons sugar	2 teaspoons melted butter
½ teaspoon salt	¼ teaspoon celery seed
¼ cup warm (105° to 110°F) water	

Heat milk in a small saucepan over medium heat until bubbles form at edge of pan; stir in shortening, sugar, and salt. Transfer to a large bowl and set aside to cool to 105° to 110°F. Meanwhile, combine warm water and yeast in a cup and set aside for yeast to soften. Grease two baking sheets.

When milk mixture has cooled, add 1¾ cups flour and the yeast mixture; stir until a soft dough forms. Turn dough out onto a work surface floured with some of remaining ¼ cup flour. Knead 5 minutes, adding as much of the flour as necessary to make a soft dough. Cover bowl and set aside in a warm place until double in size—about 30 minutes.

Divide dough in half; roll out each half to make an 8-inch round. Cut each round into 12 wedges. Brush rounds with melted butter; roll each wedge from the largest to the smallest side and place on greased baking sheet. Brush rolled dough "horns" with butter and sprinkle with celery seed. Set aside in a warm place to rise slightly—about 15 minutes.

When horns have raised slightly, preheat oven to 425°F. Bake horns until golden brown and they sound hollow when tapped on top, 10 to 12 minutes. Remove to cooling rack.

Cool 10 to 15 minutes and serve warm.

24 Servings

 "In August, according to some surveys, we waste more bread and vegetables than we do in any other month. Remember that if every family wasted only a single slice of bread a week the total would come to 100,000,000 loaves a year."—*McCall's* magazine, August 1943

YOUR COMMUNITY
can sponsor a school lunch program for its children

7

★ ★ ★ ★ Four-Star Specials ★ ★ ★ ★

CUSTARDS AND PUDDINGS

Apple Butter Custards

Baked Apple Tapioca

Baked Lemon Puddings

Chocolate Fluff

Corn Bread Pudding

Huckleberry Pudding

Indian Pudding

Lime Crumb Pudding

Party Pudding

Peanut Butter Bread Pudding

WARTIME SPECIAL

Delicious Pudding

Work on a farm...
this Summer

JOIN THE U.S. CROP CORPS

EE YOUR U.S. EMPLOYMENT SERVICE OR YOUR LOCAL COUNTY AGENT

"Now that tin is restricted wide selections of glass-packed fruits and vegetables are appearing in markets. Very pretty too. Have you begun to ask for 'glassed' foods?"—*Woman's Home Companion*, May 1942

DESSERTS THAT COULD BE assembled, baked, and served in the same dish had a lot going for them in a busy home-front kitchen. In addition, they were usually made from easy-to-find ingredients, used alternate sources of sweetness, and were an excellent way to make use of scraps of bread, the juice from canned fruit, and dried fruit. Creative combinations of whatever was in the house, these wartime standbys made it worthwhile to eat the liver and spinach so you could get to dessert. The government's frequent nutrition messages weren't forgotten when these hearty desserts were designed. Usually based on a carbohydrate for energy, they also contained milk and eggs to provide protein for strength, and often some iron-rich molasses or dried fruit. Not just add-ons, these "sweets" were an integral part of the menu, good food that moms could take pride in serving to their families.

When sugar and butter reappeared in markets after the war, and servicemen came home having known chocolate mousse, these simple custards and puddings slipped into obscurity, a sweet spot in our collective national memory. Fortunately, in the last decade or so they have been rediscovered by restaurant pastry chefs, to overwhelming acclaim. Although the recipes that follow are much lower in fat and refined sugar than today's restaurant desserts, the old-fashioned flavor makes them keepers, and the easy assembly makes them perfect for today's busy dessert makers.

 "Finely shredded tangerine peel will do wonders for more puddings and jellies than you can count."
— *S-SSH-Cooking Secrets* in *Better Homes & Gardens*, December 1943

★ ★ ★ ★ ★ Apple Butter Custards ★ ★ ★ ★ ★

Either homemade or store-bought, apple butter provides both sweetness and spice in this four-ingredient recipe. In addition to the natural sweetness of apples, which is concentrated by the process of making apple butter, added sugar in apple butter came either from the homemaker's special sugar ration allowed for canning or from a manufacturer's ration of sugar if the apple butter was purchased. A note with this recipe suggested that apple butter also be used to replace half of the sugar in pumpkin pie.

2 cups milk	⅔ cup apple butter
3 large eggs	⅛ teaspoon salt

Preheat oven to 350°F. Grease six 6-ounce custard cups; place them in a baking or roasting pan. Heat the milk in a small, heavy saucepan over low heat until bubbles form at the edge of the pan.

Meanwhile, beat the eggs in a small bowl with an electric mixer on high speed until thick and lemon colored. Beat in the apple butter and salt. Gradually beat in the milk just until smooth.

Divide the mixture into the greased custard cups. Pour boiling water into the baking pan to reach about 1 inch up the sides of the cups. Bake custards 35 to 40 minutes or until the centers appear set. Serve warm or chilled.

6 Servings

 "Cooked fruit, served hot, tastes sweeter than when cold."—*Ladies' Home Journal,* September 1942

★ ★ ★ ★ ★ Baked Apple Tapioca ★ ★ ★ ★ ★

Although tapioca is no trouble to prepare on top of the stove, you do have to watch it in order to keep it from scorching. This combination of baked apples and tapioca, two favorite family desserts, minds itself in the oven while the cook can go on to other things.

2 cups water

½ cup packed light brown sugar

⅓ cup quick-cooking tapioca

1 teaspoon cinnamon

¼ teaspoon salt

2 large red cooking apples, rinsed

1 tablespoon unsifted all-purpose
 flour

1 tablespoon butter, softened

Heavy cream or ice cream, optional

Preheat oven to 400°F. Grease a 9-inch square baking dish. Combine water, ¼ cup brown sugar, the tapioca, cinnamon, and salt in a small saucepan; bring to a boil over high heat, stirring constantly. Remove from heat.

Core unpeeled apples and slice crosswise ¼ inch thick. Arrange half of apples in greased baking dish. Pour tapioca mixture over apples. Stir together remaining ¼ cup brown sugar, the flour, and butter with a fork; spread over remaining apple rings and arrange, sugar side up, in baking dish.

Bake until apples are tender and top is lightly browned, about 30 minutes. Serve warm. Top with cream or ice cream, if desired.

6 Servings

★ ★ ★ ★ ★ Baked Lemon Puddings ★ ★ ★ ★ ★

Similar to individual little lemon pudding cakes, these tangy desserts require very little that isn't already in the house.

2 large eggs, separated

½ cup sugar

2 tablespoons butter

2 tablespoons grated lemon peel

⅛ teaspoon salt

¼ cup lemon juice

2 tablespoons unsifted all-purpose flour

1 cup milk

Preheat oven to 350°F. Grease six 6-ounce custard cups and place them in a baking or roasting pan.

Beat the egg whites in a small bowl with an electric mixer on high speed until stiff peaks form; set aside.

Beat the sugar, butter, lemon peel, and salt in a large bowl with same beaters until fluffy. Add the egg yolks, lemon juice, and flour, beating well after each addition. With the mixer on low speed, beat in the milk just until smooth. Fold in the beaten egg whites.

Divide the batter into the greased custard cups. Pour boiling water into the baking pan to reach about 1 inch up sides of cups. Bake puddings 35 to 40 minutes or until tops are golden brown. Cool 15 minutes and serve warm or refrigerate to serve chilled.

6 Servings

★ ★ ★ ★ ★ ★ # Chocolate Flupp ★ ★ ★ ★ ★ ★

This chocolate custard separates as it bakes, creating a fluffy layer on top. Desserts like this one stretched the available chocolate so that the whole family could have a share.

2 large eggs, separated

6 tablespoons granulated sugar

2 (1-ounce) squares unsweetened
   chocolate, melted

1 tablespoon butter, softened

1½ cups milk

⅓ cup unsifted all-purpose flour

½ teaspoon baking powder

⅛ teaspoon salt

Preheat oven to 375°F. Grease a shallow 1½-quart baking dish; set it in a larger baking or roasting pan.

Beat egg whites until fluffy in a small bowl. Gradually beat in 4 tablespoons sugar until stiff peaks form. With same beaters, beat egg yolks and remaining 2 tablespoons sugar in a medium bowl until thick. Beat in chocolate and butter. Add milk, flour, baking powder, and salt all at once; beat on low speed just until smooth. Fold in beaten egg whites and transfer to the greased baking dish.

Pour boiling water into the baking pan to reach about 1 inch up the sides of the dish. Bake until the center appears set, 35 to 40 minutes. Serve warm or chilled. Store any leftovers in the refrigerator.

6 Servings

★ ★ ★ ★ ★ Corn Bread Pudding ★ ★ ★ ★ ★

This concept came from a January 1944 magazine food article that offered ideas for using a basic corn bread recipe in a variety of ways. The article featured a kindly grandmother who was introduced as "a lady who learned in other war times how to be a good cook under difficulties." She told readers, "Well, we can count on corn bread!"

2 large eggs
1/3 cup packed light brown sugar
1 teaspoon ground cinnamon
1/4 teaspoon salt

2 cups milk
2 cups day-old corn bread cubes
1/4 cup dark seedless raisins

Preheat oven to 350°F. Grease a 1¹/₂-quart shallow baking dish.

Beat eggs, brown sugar, cinnamon, and salt in a medium bowl; beat in milk. Combine corn bread and raisins in greased baking dish. Pour milk mixture over bread. Bake pudding until the center appears set and top is golden brown, 45 to 50 minutes. Serve warm or chilled.

6 Servings

"Unless baked desserts are to be turned out on a serving dish, it is a good idea to bake them in casseroles or other attractive baking dishes. This saves dishes and will help keep the dessert hot."
—*Down-On-The-Farm Cook Book*, 1943

★ ★ ★ ★ ★ Huckleberry Pudding ★ ★ ★ ★ ★

This recipe was designed as a thrifty use for a product that was free for the picking in most areas. However, huckleberries are more difficult to come by these days than they were in the 1940s. If you don't have a huckleberry bush in your backyard, cultivated blueberries will do. The recipe declared it "a wholesome pudding for children."

1½ cups unsifted all-purpose flour

2 tablespoons sugar

¾ teaspoon baking soda

⅛ teaspoon salt

¾ cup light molasses

3 cups huckleberries or blueberries, rinsed and thoroughly drained

Heavy cream or ice cream, optional

Preheat oven to 350°F. Grease a 1½-quart shallow baking dish. Combine flour, sugar, soda, and salt in a large bowl; stir in molasses until thoroughly blended. Fold in huckleberries.

Spread mixture in greased baking dish and bake 30 to 35 minutes or until the top surface is firm.

Cool slightly and serve from baking dish. Top servings with a drizzle of heavy cream or a scoop of ice cream, if desired.

6 Servings

 "Each soldier who goes overseas automatically ties up 270 days supply of food. It takes that much to feed him, afloat and in the field, to allow for loss by enemy action and to keep the supply lines filled and moving."—*McCall's* magazine, August 1943

★ ★ ★ ★ ★ Indian Pudding ★ ★ ★ ★ ★

This New England favorite develops a rich, mellow flavor as the liquid reduces during slow, low-temperature baking. More butter and some granulated sugar are often added today, but this low-fat, "sugarless" wartime version provides the traditional flavor without those scarce commodities.

1 quart milk	2 teaspoons cinnamon
½ cup yellow cornmeal	½ teaspoon ground nutmeg
½ cup light molasses	¼ teaspoon salt
2 tablespoons butter	Heavy cream or ice cream, optional

Preheat oven to 325°F. Grease a 1½-quart shallow baking dish. Combine ½ cup milk and the cornmeal in a small bowl; set aside.

Heat remaining milk in a large saucepan over low heat until small bubbles begin to form at the side of the pan. Gradually beat the cornmeal mixture into the hot milk. Cook, stirring occasionally, 10 minutes. Stir in molasses, butter, cinnamon, nutmeg, and salt.

Transfer pudding to greased baking dish and bake 1 hour. Stir and smooth top surface of pudding. Bake 1 hour longer or until the top surface is firm and lightly browned.

Cool slightly and serve from baking dish. Top servings with a drizzle of heavy cream or a scoop of ice cream, if desired.

6 to 8 Servings

★ ★ ★ ★ ★ Lime Crumb Pudding ★ ★ ★ ★ ★

The original recipe for this "sugarless" dessert told homemakers that it "costs less than 2 points at most." This can also be made with lemon or orange juice and rind. If you make it with orange, you can substitute 1 cup orange juice for 1 cup of the water.

1½ cups cold water

⅓ cup honey

2 teaspoons grated lime peel

¼ cup lime juice

2 large eggs, separated

3 cups day-old bread crumbs

2 tablespoons butter, melted

Combine the water, honey, lime peel, lime juice, and egg yolks in a large bowl. Fold in the bread crumbs; set aside 15 minutes.

Preheat oven to 350°F. Grease a 2-quart shallow baking dish and place in a large baking or roasting pan.

Beat the egg whites in a small bowl with an electric mixer on high speed until soft peaks form. Fold beaten whites into the lime mixture. Transfer the lime mixture to the greased baking dish; drizzle with butter. Pour boiling water into the baking pan to reach about 1 inch up the sides of the baking dish. Bake pudding 40 to 45 minutes or until the center appears set. Serve warm or chilled.

6 Servings

"Humpty Dumpty's always on call
Bursting with vitamins for us all
Proteins and minerals, too, in his shell
What we all need to help keep us well"
—*Your Share*, 1943

★ ★ ★ ★ ★ ★ ★ Party Pudding ★ ★ ★ ★ ★ ★ ★

This quintessential bread pudding recipe is based on one that appeared in a 1944 General Mills advertisement entitled "Mealtime Magic with Enriched Bread." The three "point-saving recipes" that appeared were "Published in tribute to the wartime services of the Bakers of America." Homemakers were told that "there's magic in enriched bread…magic enough to make an over-worked ration book and a skimpy refrigerator turn out a feast!"

2 large eggs	2 cups milk
½ cup sugar	3 cups day-old bread crumbs
1 teaspoon vanilla extract	⅔ cup fruit jam
¼ teaspoon salt	

Preheat oven to 350°F. Grease a 1½-quart shallow baking dish.

Beat eggs, sugar, vanilla, and salt in a medium bowl; gradually beat in milk. Arrange bread crumbs in greased baking dish. Pour milk mixture over bread. Bake pudding 35 to 40 minutes or until the center appears set.

Remove pudding from oven; spoon jam over surface of pudding. Serve warm or chilled.

6 Servings

 "It's just as important to see that saved things are used."—Mrs. K. Weber, quoted in *Farm Journal and Farmer's Wife*, February 1943

★ ★ ★ Peanut Butter Bread Pudding ★ ★ ★

This hearty pudding would be the perfect dessert for a Victory Garden meal as the milk, peanut butter, and egg all contribute protein.

1½ cups milk

½ cup peanut butter

¼ cup sugar

1 large egg

1 teaspoon vanilla extract

3 cups day-old bread cubes

Preheat oven to 350°F. Grease a 1½-quart shallow baking dish; set it in a larger baking or roasting pan. Heat milk in a small saucepan until bubbles form at the edge of the pan.

Beat together peanut butter, sugar, egg, and vanilla in a small bowl; gradually beat in milk. Arrange bread in greased baking dish. Pour milk mixture over bread.

Bake pudding until the center appears set, 35 to 40 minutes. Serve warm or chilled. Store any leftovers in the refrigerator.

4 Servings

"Good food builds morale. And that is something which is every bit as important in wartime for those of us at home as it is for the men in the army."—*Ladies' Home Journal*, March 1942

Delicious Pudding

This canned pudding was developed for the Burpee Home Canning system, which used tin (not steel or aluminum) cans and sold a special can sealer that was similar to the system used by commercial canners. If you would like to try this unusual pudding, steam it in two 4-cup pudding molds for 90 minutes, or bake it in 2 greased 7-inch loaf pans for 40 to 45 minutes at 350°F.

3/4 cupful sour milk

1 large egg

1 cupful sugar

1 cupful grated carrots

1 cupful grated potatoes

1 teaspoonful soda

1 teaspoonful cinnamon

1/2 teaspoonful salt

1/2 teaspoonful allspice

1/2 teaspoonful nutmeg

1 1/2 cupfuls unsifted all-purpose flour

1 cup seeded or dark seedless raisins

Beat sour milk and egg until combined. Stir in sugar, carrots, potatoes, soda, cinnamon, salt, allspice, and nutmeg. Combine flour and raisins; fold into pudding mixture until combined.

Pack into cans and steam 30 minutes. Seal with can sealer and process 65 minutes in a boiling water bath.

Cool, label, and store in a cool place.

2 (2-cup) puddings

8

★ ★ ★ ★ ★ Patriotic Sweets ★ ★ ★ ★ ★

COBBLERS AND OTHER FRUIT DESSERTS

Apple-Gingerbread Cobbler

Apple Pandowdy

Apricot Betty

Berry-Buttermilk Shortcakes

Cherry Puffs

Crimson Cottage Pudding

Plum Cobbler

Quick Fruit Duff

Scalloped Rhubarb

Strawberry "Long" Cake

Whole Wheat Scallop

WARTIME SPECIAL

Lemon Dumplings

"To Whip Evaporated Milk: Milk, bowl and beater should be thoroughly chilled to about 40°F. If the milk fails to whip, it is not cold enough."—*Victory Binding of the American Woman's Cook Book*, 1942

IN 1941, AS YOUNG AMERICANS were drafted into the service and received perhaps the first medical examination of their lives, the nation began to realize the toll that the decade of depression had taken on overall health. In an effort to jump-start the recovery, the government set nutritional guidelines and assigned homemakers as "home-front warriors," to see that their families were well fed every day. Fruit and grain products were two of the important components of the recommended diet. The baked desserts that follow were promoted as good ways to combine the two in a treat that families would be happy to eat. The addition of dried fruit, molasses, an occasional egg, and some dairy products increased their nutritional value as well. Low in fat and refined sugar, these desserts make the most of the natural sugars in fruit, and use leftover bread and the reserved syrups from canned fruit in order to reduce waste. One wartime butter-saving trick that is frequently used in this chapter is the addition of a very small amount of butter to the surface of the dessert, where it will be sure to be noticed. The recipes that follow will give you a head start in meeting the requirements of the wartime "Basic Seven Food Groups" as well as today's nutritional guidelines.

 "Tests have shown Brer Rabbit Molasses is second only to liver as a rich food source of iron the body can use. . . . Three tablespoons of Brer Rabbit supply about a third of a child's minimum daily iron requirements based on government standards."—1943 advertisement

★ ★ ★ ★ Apple-Gingerbread Cobbler ★ ★ ★ ★

This harvest dessert is such a natural pairing that I am surprised I haven't seen it on today's restaurant menus.

2¼ cups unsifted all-purpose flour

2 teaspoons ground ginger

1½ teaspoons baking soda

1 teaspoon ground cinnamon

¼ teaspoon salt

¼ teaspoon ground cloves

8 medium cooking apples, peeled
 and sliced

⅓ cup light corn syrup

1 tablespoon butter, melted

1¼ cup light molasses

½ cup melted shortening

1 large egg, lightly beaten

¾ cup water

Preheat oven to 350°F. Grease a 13- by 9-inch baking dish or pan. Stir together flour, ginger, soda, cinnamon, salt, and cloves in a medium bowl.

Combine apples, corn syrup, and butter in the baking dish; spread evenly. Cover with aluminum foil and bake 20 minutes.

Meanwhile, combine molasses and shortening in a medium bowl; add egg and beat until well blended. Add the dry ingredients alternately with the water. Spoon over partially cooked apples in baking dish and bake 30 to 35 minutes.

Cool 5 minutes. Cut into 12 rectangles and serve warm from the baking dish.

12 Servings

 "Citrus-fruit juices added to fresh apples, peaches, and bananas not only prevent darkening, as you already know, but reduce loss of C—the hardest-to-keep vitamin."—*Ladies' Home Journal,* September 1942

★ ★ ★ ★ ★ ★ Apple Pandowdy ★ ★ ★ ★ ★ ★ ★

Although the topping is much like that on a cobbler, the recipe in the February 1945 issue of Woman's Home Companion, *from which this was adapted, did say, "some like to break the crust into the juicy fruit." This is what makes it a pandowdy. The method of cutting the topping into rectangles before moving it to the baking dish certainly makes the process easier.*

3 pounds (about 10 medium)
   cooking apples, peeled and sliced

½ cup packed light brown sugar

⅓ cup light molasses

1 teaspoon cornstarch

1 teaspoon ground cinnamon

¼ teaspoon ground nutmeg

2 cups unsifted all-purpose flour

¼ cup granulated sugar

4 teaspoons baking powder

¾ teaspoon salt

⅓ cup vegetable shortening or
   butter (or a mixture)

⅔ cup milk

Preheat oven to 350°F. Grease a 13- by 9-inch baking dish. Toss together apples, brown sugar, molasses, cornstarch, cinnamon, and nutmeg in a large bowl; spread out in greased baking dish.

Combine flour, sugar, baking powder, and salt in a medium bowl. Cut in shortening with a pastry blender or two knives until the mixture forms fine crumbs. Add milk and stir just until combined. Roll dough on a floured board with a floured rolling pin to a 13- by 9-inch rectangle. Cut into 8 rectangles and transfer onto apple mixture.

Bake until the apples are tender and crust is golden, 35 to 45 minutes. Cool 15 minutes. Break up crust into apple mixture and serve from pan, or invert biscuit rectangles on serving plates and spoon apple filling on top.

8 Servings

★ ★ ★ ★ ★ ★ ★ Apricot Betty ★ ★ ★ ★ ★ ★ ★

Dried apricots were easily available in America during the war and were used to bring big flavor as well as added nutrition to desserts. I look back fondly on an era when desserts were considered good for you.

1 cup dried apricot halves, quartered

½ cup boiling apple juice or water

⅓ cup dark corn syrup

1 teaspoon ground cinnamon

2½ cups day-old, firm white bread cubes (5 or 6 slices bread)

1 teaspoon butter, melted

1 large egg white

⅛ teaspoon cornstarch

¼ cup light corn syrup

Combine apricots and apple juice in a large bowl; set aside 15 minutes. Lightly grease a 1½-quart casserole or baking dish.

Preheat oven to 350°F. Stir dark corn syrup and cinnamon into apricot mixture; fold in bread cubes. Transfer mixture to greased casserole; drizzle butter over top. Bake until surface is brown—20 to 25 minutes.

Meanwhile, combine egg white and cornstarch in a small bowl. Beat at high speed until it begins to hold soft peaks. Very gradually beat in corn syrup until mixture is stiff. Spread over surface of Betty and bake 10 minutes longer or until the meringue is brown and hot throughout.

Cool 5 to 10 minutes on a wire rack, then serve warm from the casserole.

6 Servings

 "Harping on thrift makes wrinkles and a rebellious family. Be smooth, and make thrift attractive."—*Farm Journal and Farmer's Wife*, February 1943

★ ★ ★ ★ Berry-Buttermilk Shortcakes ★ ★ ★ ★

These biscuit shortcakes are good with whatever berry is in season, or with a mixture of berries. If you are using strawberries and they are more than 3/4 inch in diameter, halve or quarter them so they will be easier to serve. In the 1940s, this versatile recipe was made with home-canned cherries or apple slices when berry season was over and was converted to a meat-saving main dish shortcake by spooning a chicken or pork and vegetable stew over the biscuits.

2 cups unsifted all-purpose flour	1/2 cup buttermilk
1 tablespoon granulated sugar	1 large egg, beaten
3 teaspoons baking powder	1 tablespoon milk
1/4 teaspoon baking soda	4 cups small berries
1/4 teaspoon salt	2 tablespoons confectioners' sugar
1/3 cup vegetable shortening or butter (or a mixture)	2 cups sweetened whipped cream

Preheat oven to 425°F. Lightly grease a baking sheet.

Combine flour, sugar, baking powder, soda, and salt in a medium bowl. Cut in shortening with a pastry blender or two knives until the mixture forms coarse crumbs.

Combine the buttermilk and egg; add to dry ingredients and stir together just until combined. Turn dough out onto a floured board and knead into a ball. Roll out to 1/2-inch thickness. Cut out twelve 3-inch rounds, rerolling if necessary. Place 6 rounds on greased baking sheet; top each round with another round. Brush tops with milk and bake for 12 to 15 minutes or until lightly browned. Cool 15 minutes on baking sheet.

Meanwhile, combine the berries with the confectioners' sugar. To serve, place biscuits on dessert plates, split where the biscuits were set together. Spoon about two-thirds of berries over bottom biscuits. Replace top biscuits and spoon on remaining berries and the whipped cream.

6 Servings

★ ★ ★ ★ ★ ★ ★ Cherry Puffs ★ ★ ★ ★ ★ ★ ★

During the war most commercially canned sour cherries went to the armed services for cherry pies, but their high acidity made cherries a favorite with home canners who found them easy to successfully preserve.

1 pint pitted canned sour cherries in heavy syrup, see Note

3/4 teaspoon almond extract

1/3 cup sugar

1/4 cup vegetable shortening or butter (or a mixture)

1 large egg

1/4 teaspoon salt

3/4 cup unsifted all-purpose flour

1/2 cup milk

1 1/2 teaspoons baking powder

1 tablespoon cornstarch

1 tablespoon lemon juice

Preheat oven to 375°F. Grease six 6-ounce custard cups; place them in a baking or roasting pan. Drain the cherries well, reserving syrup. Combine the cherries and 1/4 teaspoon almond extract; divide cherries into custard cups.

Beat sugar, shortening, egg, remaining 1/2 teaspoon almond extract, and the salt until fluffy. Add flour, milk, and baking powder all at once; beat just until smooth. Divide the batter onto the cherries in the custard cups and bake until the centers spring back when lightly pressed, 30 to 35 minutes.

Meanwhile, combine 3/4 cup syrup from cherries (add light corn syrup if there wasn't enough syrup in the can or jar), the cornstarch, and lemon juice in a small saucepan. Bring to a boil, stirring constantly, and cook 1 minute.

To serve, loosen sides of puffs from cups and invert onto serving plates. Top with cherry sauce.

NOTE: If your cherries are packed in water, toss drained cherries with 1/4 cup sugar before dividing and sweeten sauce to taste.

12 Servings

★ ★ ★ ★ Crimson Cottage Pudding ★ ★ ★ ★

The cake for this cottage pudding is so simple that it doesn't even require an egg. The sauce can be made from any flavor of jam or jelly. Another wartime trick was to top cottage pudding with the thickened sugar syrup saved when draining canned fruit, particularly canned plums.

2 cups sifted cake flour (sift before measuring)

2½ teaspoons baking powder

¼ teaspoon salt

3 tablespoons vegetable shortening or butter (or a mixture)

½ cup light corn syrup

¾ cup milk

2 teaspoons vanilla extract

Crimson Sauce (recipe follows)

Preheat oven to 350°F. Grease a 9-inch square baking pan. Sift or stir together the flour, baking powder, and salt.

Beat the shortening with an electric mixer on high speed until fluffy; gradually beat in the corn syrup. Add the dry ingredients, milk, and vanilla; beat on low speed just until smooth.

Spoon the batter into the prepared pan and bake 25 to 30 minutes or until the center springs back when lightly pressed. Meanwhile, prepare Crimson Sauce.

Cool pudding in pan 5 minutes. Cut into 9 squares; remove squares to serving plates, top with Crimson Sauce and serve warm.

Crimson Sauce: In a small saucepan, heat together ⅔ cup seedless red raspberry jam and 2 tablespoons lemon juice just until jam melts.

9 Servings

★ ★ ★ ★ ★ ★ ★ Plum Cobbler ★ ★ ★ ★ ★ ★ ★

This harvest recipe comes from a fall 1944 magazine article reminding bakers just how easy and flavorful "old-fashioned" cobblers can be. If plums are out of season, you can substitute home- or commercially canned plums and use the syrup from the jar for the sauce.

2 pounds (about 4 cups) Italian
    plums, rinsed, seeded, and
    quartered, *see Note*
1/2 cup sugar
1 tablespoon cornstarch
1 teaspoon grated lemon peel
2 tablespoons lemon juice

1 1/4 cups unsifted all-purpose flour
2 teaspoons baking powder
1/4 teaspoon salt
1/4 cup vegetable shortening or
    butter (or a mixture)
1/2 cup milk
1 large egg, lightly beaten

Preheat oven to 350°F. Grease a 9-inch square baking dish. Combine the plums, 1/4 cup sugar, the cornstarch, lemon peel, and lemon juice in a large bowl; spread out in greased baking dish.

Combine flour, remaining 1/4 cup sugar, the baking powder, and salt in a medium bowl. Cut in shortening with a pastry blender or two knives until the mixture forms fine crumbs. Add milk and egg; stir just until combined. Spoon over plums.

Bake cobbler 30 to 35 minutes or until the center springs back when lightly pressed.

Cool 15 minutes. Cut into 6 rectangles and serve from pan.

NOTE: You can substitute two (1-pound) cans of plums. Drain plums reserving the syrup. Remove seeds, quarter plums and combine them with 3/4 cup syrup from the cans, the cornstarch, lemon peel, and lemon juice from the recipe. You won't need the 1/4 cup sugar called for with the fresh plums.

6 Servings

★ ★ ★ ★ ★ ★ Quick Fruit Duff ★ ★ ★ ★ ★ ★

Although other mixes had been developed for the armed services and would appear in retail stores after the war, only biscuit mix and gingerbread mix were widely advertised for the home baker. This quick dessert was a preview of what was to come in the 1950s.

1 quart canned apricots, berries, cherries, peaches, or pears

2 tablespoons water

1 tablespoon lemon juice

1 tablespoon cornstarch

1 cup commercial biscuit mix

3 tablespoons packed light brown sugar

$\frac{1}{3}$ cup milk

1 tablespoon butter, melted

$\frac{1}{8}$ teaspoon ground nutmeg

Preheat oven to 425°F. Grease a shallow 1½-quart baking dish. Drain fruit, reserving syrup; place fruit in baking dish.

Combine the water, lemon juice, and cornstarch in a small saucepan until smooth. Gradually stir in ¾ cup reserved syrup from fruit (if you don't have enough add light corn syrup to make ¾ cup.) Bring mixture to a boil and pour over fruit.

Combine biscuit mix and brown sugar in a small bowl; stir in milk. Spoon biscuit mixture over fruit; drizzle with butter and sprinkle with nutmeg. Bake until top is golden and the filling bubbles, 25 to 30 minutes.

Cool 5 minutes. Cut into 6 rectangles and serve warm from the baking dish.

6 Servings

" 'Nutrition' has to be sold to the family, but not by strong-arm methods. Men and children will not eat food because it is 'good for them'—unless they like it."—*Coupon Cookery*, 1943

★ ★ ★ ★ ★ ★ Scalloped Rhubarb ★ ★ ★ ★ ★ ★

Fresh rhubarb in the garden was a welcome sign of spring for wartime bakers, but jars of rhubarb in the cellar meant you could enjoy this "scalloped" or layered dessert all year long. These days, you are more likely to have frozen than canned rhubarb when the fresh is not available, but if you do have home-canned rhubarb, it's still a time saver. Take a look at the Note following the recipe for directions on using it.

1¼ pounds fresh rhubarb, trimmed, rinsed, and cut into 1-inch pieces (2 cups pieces), or 2 cups frozen rhubarb, see Note

⅓ cup granulated sugar

¼ cup water

2 teaspoons cornstarch

4 cups day-old white bread crumbs

¼ cup packed light brown sugar

3 tablespoons butter, melted

1 teaspoon grated lemon peel

Combine rhubarb, granulated sugar and 2 tablespoons water in a small saucepan; cover and bring to a boil over low heat, about 5 minutes. Combine cornstarch and remaining 2 tablespoons water; stir into rhubarb mixture. Cook, stirring until thickened; set aside.

Meanwhile, preheat oven to 400°F. Grease an 8-inch square baking dish or pan.

Combine crumbs, brown sugar, butter, and lemon peel in a small bowl. Layer ½ of crumbs, the rhubarb mixture, and remaining ½ of crumbs in greased baking dish.

Bake, uncovered, until rhubarb bubbles and crumbs have browned, 20 to 25 minutes. Cut into 4 squares and serve warm from the baking dish.

NOTE: To use canned rhubarb (rather than fresh or frozen), drain 1 pint canned rhubarb, reserving 1/2 cup syrup. In place of the simmered mixture of fresh or frozen rhubarb, sugar, and water in the above recipe, combine your drained canned rhubarb and the 1/2 cup reserved syrup directly with the cornstarch. Cook the mixture, stirring constantly, until thickened and use as directed above.

4 Servings

★ ★ ★ ★ Strawberry "Long" Cake ★ ★ ★ ★

This concept was the star of a Gold Medal Flour advertisement in the early summer of 1945. Betty Crocker told homemakers that it was so named because it made strawberries "go a long, long way." She added that, "this 'strawberry-stretcher' gives you 8 to 10 luscious servings from only one quart of berries."

1 quart small strawberries, hulled, rinsed and drained

²/₃ cup sugar

Crumb Topping, recipe follows

2 cups unsifted all-purpose flour

4 teaspoons baking powder

¹/₄ teaspoon salt

¹/₃ cup vegetable shortening or butter (or a mixture)

³/₄ cup milk

1 large egg, beaten

Heavy cream, optional

Combine strawberries and ¹/₃ cup sugar in a medium bowl; set aside. Preheat oven to 400°F. Generously grease a 12- by 7-inch rectangular (or 9-inch square) baking dish. Prepare Crumb Topping.

Combine flour, remaining ¹/₃ cup sugar, the baking powder, and salt in a medium bowl. Cut in shortening with a pastry blender or two knives until the mixture forms coarse crumbs.

Combine the milk and egg in a measuring cup or small bowl; add to dry ingredients and stir together just until all flour has been moistened and a soft dough forms. Spread dough into greased baking dish. Top with strawberries and juice. Sprinkle Crumb Topping over all.

Bake for 35 to 40 minutes or until lightly browned and bubbly.

Cool 5 minutes on wire rack. Cut into squares and serve warm with cream, if desired.

Crumb Topping: Stir together ¹/₃ cup all-purpose flour, 2 tablespoons sugar, and 1 tablespoon butter, softened, in a small bowl with a fork until crumbs form.

8 to 10 Servings

★ ★ ★ ★ ★ Whole Wheat Scallop ★ ★ ★ ★ ★

Fruit "scallops" were frequently listed in wartime menus as a weekday dessert. They were layered fruit desserts, usually with a sweetened bread-crumb topping. They could be made with either fresh or canned fruit and baked along with the casserole, loaf, or stew that was the evening's main dish, to conserve energy. Apple Scallop would probably have been a more enticing name for this one.

4 medium cooking apples, peeled
  and sliced

½ cup dark seedless raisins

1½ cups day-old whole wheat bread
  crumbs

⅓ cup sugar

1 teaspoon grated lemon peel

¼ teaspoon salt

3 tablespoons butter, melted

Preheat oven to 350°F. Grease a 9-inch square baking dish or pan.

Layer half of apples and half of raisins in the baking dish; repeat with remaining apples and raisins. Cover with aluminum foil and bake 20 minutes.

Meanwhile, combine crumbs, sugar, lemon peel, and salt in a medium bowl; add butter and toss until well blended. Spoon crumbs over partially cooked apples in baking dish and bake, uncovered, until apples are tender and crumbs have browned, 10 to 15 minutes.

Cool 5 minutes. Cut into 9 rectangles and serve warm from the baking dish.

9 Servings

 "The first semester that hot lunches were served in one Indiana school, the 113 pupils gained half a ton in weight; soaking up vitamins and body-building foods that kids seldom find in paper bags and lunch pails."— *The Saturday Evening Post,* July 4, 1942

Lemon Dumplings

Here's a dessert that could be made when there was almost nothing in the pantry. Biscuit-dough dumplings bake in a bubbling lemon mixture as it turns into a tangy sauce to be served over the dessert.

1³/₄ cups plus 2 tablespoons unsifted all-purpose flour

2 tablespoons packed light brown sugar

4 teaspoons baking powder

¹/₂ teaspoon salt

¹/₄ cup vegetable shortening or butter (or a mixture)

²/₃ cup milk

2 to 3 teaspoons grated lemon peel

¹/₄ cup lemon juice

1 cup light corn syrup

1 cup boiling water

Heat oven to 375°F. Grease a 13- by 9-inch baking dish or pan.

Combine 1³/₄ cups flour, brown sugar, baking powder, and salt in a medium bowl. Cut in shortening with a pastry blender or two knives until the mixture forms coarse crumbs. Stir milk into dry ingredients just until all dry ingredients have been moistened. Spoon into greased baking dish to make 12 drop biscuits, leaving space between the biscuits.

In same bowl, whisk together lemon peel, lemon juice, and 2 tablespoons flour until flour is completely incorporated. Beat in corn syrup and then boiling water. Pour mixture around biscuits.

Bake until biscuits have browned and sauce is bubbling, 20 to 25 minutes. Serve warm from baking dish.

9 Servings

YOUR COMMUNITY

can use many ways

to teach family food needs

Sources

American Cookery (magazine). January 1940 through December 1945.

Anderson, Jean. *The American Century Cookbook.* New York: Clarkson N. Potter, 1997.

Anderson, Karen. *Wartime Women: Sex Roles, Family Relations, and the Status of Women During World War II.* Westport, Conn.: Greenwood Press, 1981.

Bakers' Helper (magazine). *The Book of Cookies: Recipes and Sales Ideas.* Chicago: Bakers' Helper Co., 1940.

Berolzheimer, Ruth, ed. *Victory Binding of the American Woman's Cook Book.* Chicago: Consolidated Book Publishers, 1942.

Better Homes and Gardens (magazine), January 1940 through December 1945.

Blum, John Morton. *V Was for Victory: Politics and American Culture During World War II.* New York: Harcourt Brace Jovanovich, 1976.

Brinkley, David. *Washington Goes to War: The Extraordinary Story of the Transformation of a City and a Nation.* New York: Ballantine Books, 1988.

Brokaw, Tom. *The Greatest Generation.* New York: Random House, 1998.

Campbell, D'Ann. *Women at War with America: Private Lives in a Patriotic Era.* Cambridge: Harvard University Press, 1984.

Casdorph, Paul D. *Let the Good Times Roll: Life at Home in America During WWII.* New York: Paragon House, 1991.

Case, Elizabeth and Martha Wyman. *Cook's Away: A Collection of Simple Rules, Helpful Facts, and Choice Recipes Designed to Make Cooking Easy.* New York: Longmans, Green and Co., 1943.

Crocker, Betty. *Your Share: How to prepare appetizing, healthful meals with foods available today.* Minneapolis: General Mills, 1943.

Den Dooven, K. Camille. *Hamilton Ross Modern Cook Book.* Chicago: Hamilton Ross, 1940.

Farm Journal and Farmer's Wife (magazine), January 1943 through December 1943.

Fisher, Ida, ed. *Food As We Like It*. West Springfield, Mass.: Eastern States Farmers' Exchange, 1943.

Frigidaire Corporation. *Wartime Suggestions to help you get the most out of your Refrigerator*. Dayton: General Motors, 1943.

General Foods Corporation Consumer Service Department. *All About Home Baking*. New York: General Foods, 1937

Gifford, Marie. *69 Ration Recipes for Meat from Marie Gifford's Kitchen*. Chicago: Armour and Company, 1942.

Gluck, Sherna Berger, ed. *Rosie the Riveter Revisited: Women and the World War II Experience*. Boston: Twayne, 1987.

Good Housekeeping (magazine), January 1940 through December 1945.

Goodwin, Doris Kearns. *No Ordinary Time: Franklin and Eleanor Roosevelt: The Home Front in World War II*. New York: Touchstone, 1994.

Hackney, Mrs. G. Edgar, comp. *Dining for Moderns*. Edited by Ann R. Silver. New York: New York Exchange for Women's Work, 1940.

Hartmann, Susan. *The Homefront and Beyond: American Women in the 1940s*. Boston: Twayne, 1982.

Honey, Maureen. *Creating Rosie the Riveter: Class, Gender and Propaganda During World War II*. Amherst: University of Massachusetts Press, 1984.

Home Service Bureau, The. *Biscuits and Breads*. Baltimore: The Gas & Electric Company, March 1945.

———. *Home Canning and Preserving Simplified*. Baltimore: The Gas & Electric Company, July 1939.

Hoopes, Roy. *Americans Remember the Home Front: An Oral Narrative*. New York: Hawthorne Books, Inc., 1977.

———. *When the Stars Went to War: Hollywood and World War II*. New York: Random House, 1994.

Hyde, Lt. Col. E. A. *Army Mess Management Simplified*. Fort Bliss, Texas: E. A. Hyde, 1942

Kennett, Lee. *For the Duration: The United States Goes to War, Pearl Harbor–1942*. New York: Charles Scribners' Sons, 1985.

Ladies' Home Journal (magazine), January 1940 through December 1945.

Lingeman, Richard R. *Don't You Know There's a War On?: The American Home Front, 1941–1945*. New York: G.P. Putnam's Sons, 1970.

McCall's (magazine), January 1940 through December 1945.

New York State Bureau of Milk Publicity. *Victory Meal Planner*. Albany: New York, 1942.

O'Brien, Kenneth Paul and Lynn Hudson Parsons, eds. *The Home-Front War: World War II and American Society*. Westport, Conn.: Greenwood Press, 1995.

O'Neill, William L. *A Democracy at War: America's Fight at Home & Abroad in World War II.* Cambridge, Mass.: Harvard University Press, 1993.

Penny, Prudence. *Coupon Cookery.* Hollywood, Calif.: Murray & Gee, 1943.

Procter and Gamble Co. *Recipes for Good Eating,* 1945.

Rupp, Leila. *Mobilizing Women for War: German and American Propaganda, 1939–1945.* Princeton, N.J.: Princeton University Press, 1978.

Servel, Inc. Peacetime Manufacturers of the Servel Gas Refrigerator. *Eating for Fitness: Home Volunteer's Guide to Better Nutrition,* 1943.

Standard Brands. *The Bread Basket: For the times you bake at home...dozens of tested, easy recipes for fresh breads, rolls and desserts made better with Fleischmann's Yeast.* New York: Standard Brands, 1942.

Tuttle, William M., Jr. *Daddy's Gone to War: The Second World War in the Lives of America's Children.* New York: Oxford University Press, 1993.

Ward, Barbara M., ed. *Produce & Conserve, Share & Play Square: The Grocer & the Consumer on the Home-Front Battlefield During World War II.* Portsmouth, N.H.: Strawbery Banke Museum, 1994.

Weatherford, Doris. *American Women and World War II.* New York: Facts on File, 1990.

Welsh, Sarah Francis. *Western Maryland Dairy Cookbook.* Baltimore: Western Maryland Dairy.

Woman's Home Companion (magazine), January 1940 through December 1945.

Art Credits

The illustrations in this book were published by the U.S. Government Printing Office during the early 1940s and are in the public domain. They have been reproduced courtesy of the Northwestern University Library. See http://www.library.northwestern.edu/govpub/collections/wwii-posters/index.html for more information on the university's poster database.

Page xiv. *Do with less—so they'll have enough! Rationing gives you your fair share.* U.S. Office of War Information poster no. 37. Distributed by the Division of Public Inquiries (Washington, 1943).

Page xviii. *Where our men are fighting, our food is fighting. Buy wisely—cook carefully—store carefully—use leftovers.* U.S. Office of War Information poster no. 35. Distributed by the Division of Public Inquiries (Washington, 1943).

Page 2. *"Of course I can! I'm as patriotic as can be—And ration points won't worry me!"* Illustration by Dick Williams. U.S. War Food Administration (1944).

Page 10. *Keep the Home Front Pledge: Pay no more than Ceiling Prices: Pay your Points in full.* Illustration by Fred G. Cooper. U.S. Office of Price Administration (Washington, 1944).

Page 17. *Grow Your Own: Be Sure!* Illustration by Grover Strong. U.S. Government Printing Office (Washington, 1945?).

Page 28. Sheet of eight 1-pound sugar allowance coupons. Office of Price Administration form no. R-327 (Washington, 194?).

Page 32. *Food is a weapon. Don't waste it! Buy wisely—cook carefully—eat it all.* U.S. Office of War Information poster no. 58. Distributed by the Division of Public Inquiries (Washington, 1943).

Page 47. *Rationing means a fair share for all of us.* Illustration by Herbert Roese. U.S. Office of Price Administration (Washington, 1943).

Page 48. *We'll have lots to eat this winter, won't we Mother? Grow your own. Can your own.* Illustration by Alfred Parker. U.S. Office of War Information poster no. 57. Distributed by the Division of Public Inquires (Washington, 1943).

Page 50. *Can all you can. It's a real war job!* U.S. Office of War Information poster no. 77. Distributed by the Division of Public Inquiries (Washington, 1943).

Page 68. *Every child needs a good school lunch. The War Food Administration will help your community start a school lunch program.* U.S. War Food Administration (Washington, 1943).

Page 70. *Sugar is scarce. Make it stretch.* Illustration by Robbins-Tilley. U.S. Office of Price Administration (Washington, 1946).

Page 87. *Milk and eggs—nature's food: clean, covered, cold—will stay good!* U.S. Bureau of Home Economics (Washington, 1942).

Page 92. *He eats a ton a year. Your farm can help.* U.S. War Food Administration (Washington, 1942).

Page 107. *Pitch in and help! Join the Women's Land Army of the U.S. Crop Corps.* Illustration by Hubert Morley. U.S. Extension Service (Washington, 1942).

Page 114. *Cost of living 1918, 1944.* U.S. Office of Price Administration (Washington, 1944).

Page 123. *Rationing safeguards your share.* U.S. Office of Price Administration (Washington, 1942).

Page 134. *You can learn best ways to can and store the foods you need.* U.S. Extension Service. Make America Strong series no. 8 (Washington, 1941).

Page 138. *Your community can sponsor a school lunch program for its children.* U.S. Extension Service. Make America Strong series no. 10 (Washington, 1941).

Page 140. *Work on a farm—this summer. Join the U.S. Crop Corps.* Illustration by Spencer Douglass Crockwell. U.S. Office of War Information poster no. 59 (Washington, 1943).

Page 154. *That tired feeling: Rx, regular rest and sleep, good food, recreation.* Illustration by Nydorf. U.S. Public Health Service. Workers health poster no. 30 (Washington, 1944).

Page 168. *Your community can use many ways to teach family food needs.* U.S. Extension Service. Make America Strong series no. 11 (Washington, 1941).

Page 172. *For work, for play, 3 "squares" a day. Eat the basic 7 way.* Illustration by Ted Jung. U.S. War Food Administration (Washington, 1944).

Index

★ **INDEX** ★

Notes